OLSAT™
TEST PREP
GRADE 3

OLSAT® TEST PREP GRADE 3
Level D

Gateway Gifted Resources™
www.GatewayGifted.com

PLEASE LEAVE US A REVIEW!

Thank you for selecting this book. We are a family-owned publishing company - a consortium of educators, book designers, illustrators, parents, and kid-testers.

We would be thrilled if you left us a quick review on the website where you purchased this book!

The Gateway Gifted Resources™ Team
www.GatewayGifted.com

TABLE OF CONTENTS

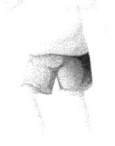

INTRODUCTION

ABOUT THIS BOOK: This book helps prepare children for the OLSAT® Level D, a test given to third graders. Not only will this publication help prepare children for the OLSAT®, these logic-based exercises may also be used for other gifted test preparation and as critical thinking exercises. This book has four parts.

1. **Introduction:** About this book & the OLSAT®, Test Taking Tips, Points Tracking, and Question Examples

2. **Practice Test 1 (Workbook Format):** These pages are designed similarly to content tested in the OLSAT®'s 15 test question types. Questions are grouped by question type, so that your child can more easily comprehend question material.

Unless your child already has experience with OLSAT® prep materials, you should complete Practice Test 1 (Workbook Format) together with no time limit. **Before doing this section with your child, read the Question Examples & Explanations.**

3. **Practice Test 2 & Practice Test 3:** These help children develop critical thinking and test-taking skills. It provides an introduction to standardized testing in a relaxed manner (parents provide guidance if needed) and an opportunity for children to focus on a group of questions for a longer time period. This part is also a way for parents to identify points of strength/ challenges.

Questions in Practice Test 2 & 3 are not grouped by question type. When your child takes the test, questions will most likely not be grouped by question type.

4. **Answer Keys:** This has the answers to Practice Test 1, 2, and 3 as well as brief answer explanations.

ABOUT THE OLSAT® LEVEL D

- The OLSAT® Level D is given to children in third grade.
- It has 64 questions in multiple choice format.
- The test lasts approximately 50 minutes.
- Schools use the test for admittance to gifted/advanced programs.
- Questions are different than those found on typical grade level quizzes, tests, and standardized testing.
- Here are the three OLSAT® Level D question types and corresponding question sections:

    -Verbal: Antonyms, Sentence Completion, Sentence Arrangement, Arithmetic Reasoning, Verbal Analogies, Verbal Classification, Logical Selection, Word/Letter Matrix

    -Non Verbal: Figure Analogies, Figure Classification, Figure Series, Pattern Matrix

    -Quantitative: Numeric Inferences, Numeric Matrix, Numeric Series

ABOUT OLSAT® TESTING PROCEDURES: These vary by school. Tests may be given individually or in a group. These tests may be used as the single factor for admission to gifted programs, or they may be used in combination with IQ tests or as part of a student "portfolio." They are used by some schools together with tests like Iowa Assessments™. Check with your testing site to determine its specific testing procedures.

QUESTION NOTE: Because each child has different cognitive abilities, the questions in this book are at varied skill levels. The exercises may or may not require a great deal of parental guidance to complete, depending on your child's abilities, prior test prep experience, or prior testing experience. Most sections of Practice Test 1 begin with a relatively easy question. We suggest always completing at least the first question together, ensuring your child is not confused about what the question asks or with the directions.

SCORING NOTE: Check with your school for its scoring procedure and admissions requirements. Here is a general summary of the OLSAT® scoring process. First, your child's raw score is established. This is the number of questions correctly answered. Points are not deducted for questions answered incorrectly. Next, this score is compared to other test-takers of his/her same age group to then calculate your child's percentile rank. If your child achieved the percentile rank of 98%, then (s)he scored as well as or better than 98% of test-takers. Note that a percentile rank "score" cannot be obtained from our practice material. This material has not been given to a large enough sample of test-takers to develop any kind of base score necessary for percentile rank calculations.

TEST TAKING TIPS
- **Be sure your child looks carefully at each answer choice.** OLSAT® questions can be quite challenging. Even if your child thinks (s)he knows the answer - (s)he should look at each choice.
- **Test-takers receive points for the number of correct answers.** If your child says that (s)he does not know the answer, (s)he should first eliminate any answers that are clearly incorrect. Guess instead of leaving a question blank.
- **In Practice Test 1, go through the exercises together by talking about them:** what the exercise is asking the child to do and what makes the answer choices correct/incorrect. This will familiarize your child with working through exercises and will help to develop a process of elimination (getting rid of incorrect answer choices).
- **Remember common sense tips like getting enough sleep.** It has been scientifically proven that kids perform below their grade level when tired. **Feed them a breakfast for sustained energy and concentration** (complex carbohydrates and protein; avoid foods/drinks high in sugar). Have them use the restroom prior to the test.

POINTS TRACKING
To increase child engagement and to add an incentive to complete book exercises, a game theme accompanies this book. As your child completes the three Practice Tests, (s)he earns 1 point per page.

After completing all pages, they will have earned 64 points. Some parents may want to offer a special treat as well for completion, although this is at the parent's discretion.

WE NEED <u>YOUR</u> HELP!

We've got a challenge for you! Are you up for it?

This book is filled with mind-bending, challenging questions, and we need your help to answer them.

For every page you do, you earn 1 point.

So far, the highest score anyone has ever earned is 64 points. Do you have what it takes to earn 64? Use the space below to track your points.

CAN YOU EARN 64 POINTS?

The questions start on page 6. Your parent (or other adult) will let you know what you need to do. Remember to:

- try to answer the questions the right way (instead of trying to finish really fast)
- pay attention
- look closely at all choices before choosing an answer
- keep trying even if some questions are hard

POINTS TRACKING

Date	Points	Date	Points	Date	Points
_____	_____	_____	_____	_____	_____
_____	_____	_____	_____	_____	_____

QUESTION EXAMPLES & EXPLANATIONS

This section introduces the 15 question types on the OLSAT® Level D using <u>basic</u> examples and explanations.

VERBAL SECTION

<u>1. Antonyms</u>
Directions: Read the sentence and choose which word is the opposite of the word in quotation marks.

The opposite of "best" is _____.

A. slow   B. bad   C. worst   D. great

The opposite of "best" is "worst." This section tests a student's vocabulary and their ability to reason and recognize a word's true opposite. In the example above, some students may choose "bad," when "worst" is actually the true opposite. Be sure to carefully go through the choices to pick the true opposite.

<u>2. Sentence Completion</u>
Directions: Read the sentence. There is a missing word. Which answer choice goes best in the sentence?

If you are not _____ with the vase, it will break.

A. careless   B. careful   C. clear   D. risky

The answer is B. Here, be sure to pay attention to each word in the sentence. After choosing your answer, reread the sentence together with your answer choice. Pay attention for "negative" words like "not." Also pay attention for "contrasting" words like "however," "but," "despite," that can be used to show contrasting ideas in sentences.

<u>3. Sentence Arrangement</u>
Directions: The words below need to be arranged to make the best sentence. Which letter would the <u>first</u> word of the sentence begin with? Here are the words:

yummy   for   waited   puppies   a   treat   the   two

A. W   B. T   C. P   D. Y

The correct sentence is: The two puppies waited for a yummy treat. The answer is B. Here are some tips.
1- Finding the main subject and verb will help you establish the basic structure. First, identify the verb(s). This will give you a clue to the subject. Then, try to identify the subject. Some sentences will have more than one noun that could be the subject. If there is more than one noun, test each one.
2- Group related words: Identify phrases or groups of words that belong together (e.g., adjectives with nouns, adverbs with verbs). This can help you see how parts of the sentence connect.
3- Look for clues: Some sentences may have words that indicate time (e.g., "yesterday," "now"), conjunctions (e.g., "and," "but"), or prepositions (e.g., "in," "on") that provide context and help you organize the sentence.

<u>4. Arithmetic Reasoning</u>   Directions: Read the question then choose your answer.

Julia and Mike had pizza for lunch. Julia ate 7 slices. Mark ate 2 more slices than Julia. How many slices did they eat all together?
A. 9   B. 7   C. 16   D. 12

First, find the number Mark ate. He ate 2 more than Julia, so 2 + 7 = 9. Mark at 9 slices. Julia ate 7 slices. So, 9+7 = 16. These questions are not a test so much of math abilities. They are an assessment of your child's ability to read word problems, turn the words into equations, and solve the equations.

5. Logical Selection   Directions: Read the sentence and choose which word best completes the sentence.

A lake must have _____.

A. boats   B. fish   C. swimmers   D. water

The answer is water. Here, you need to use logic and reasoning to figure out which choice is the only one that is truly needed.

6. Verbal Analogies
Directions: Look at the first set of words. Try to figure out how they belong together. Next, look at the second set of words. The answer is missing. Figure out which answer choice would make the second set go together in the same way that the first set goes together.

toe > foot : petal > ?   A. stem   B. bee   C. leg   D. flower

The answer is D. Here are some strategies to help arrive at the correct answer:
• Try to come up with a "rule" describing how the first set goes together. Take this rule, apply it to the first word in the second set. Which answer choice makes the second set follow the same "rule?" If more than one choice works, you need a more specific rule. Here, a "rule" for the first set is that "the first word (toe) is part of the second word (foot)." In the next set, using this rule, "flower" is the answer. A petal is part of a flower.
• Another strategy is to come up with a sentence describing how the first set of words go together. A sentence would be: A toe is part of a foot. Then, take this sentence and apply it to the word in the second set: A petal is part of a ?. Figure out which answer choice would best complete the sentence. (It would be "flower.")
• Do not choose a word simply because it *has to do with* the first set. For example, choice A ("stem") *has to do with* a petal, but does not follow the rule.

Here are more simple examples. Read the "Question" then "Answer Choices" to your child. Which choice goes best? (The answer is underlined.)

Analogy Logic	Question	Answer Choices (Answer is Underlined)			
• Antonyms	On *is to* Off -as- Hot *is to* _?_	Warm	Sun	Cold	Oven
• Synonyms	Big *is to* Large -as- Horrible *is to* _?_	Tired	Stale	Sour	Awful
• Whole: Part	Tree *is to* Branch -as- House *is to* _?_	Street	Apartment	Room	Home
• Degree	Good *is to* Excellent -as- Tired *is to* _?_	Boring	Exhausted	Drowsy	Slow
• Object: Location	Sun *is to* Sky -as- Swing *is to* _?_	Playground	Monkey Bars	Sidewalk	Grass
• Object: Creator	Painting *is to* Artist -as- Furniture *is to* _?_	Carpenter	Tool	Chair	Potter
• Object: Container	Ice Cube *is to* Ice Tray -as- Flower *is to* _?_	Petal	Vase	Smell	Florist
• Object: 3D Shape	Ball *is to* Sphere -as- Dice *is to* _?_	Line	Square	Cone	Cube
• Object: Location Used	Jet *is to* Sky -as- Canoe *is to* _?_	Boat	Paddle	Water	Sail

7. Verbal Classification
Directions: These words all go together in a certain way except for one. Which word does not go with the others?

A. fork   B. chopsticks   C. knife   D. meat   E. spoon

Here, D is the answer. All the others are utensils used for eating. However, meat is a kind of food. Even though meat has to do with food, it is not like the others.

Try to come up with a "rule" describing how the words are alike, except for one. If more than one choice does not follow the rule, then try a more specific rule.

More examples are on the next page.

Read the list of 5 words to your child, then ask which does not belong.
The gray text lists the question's logic. The underlined text is the word that does not belong.

- function and uses of common objects (i.e., writing and drawing / measuring / cutting / drinking / eating)
Fork / Chopsticks / Knife / Meat / Spoon   (Utensils Used For Eating)

- location of common objects
Refrigerator / Shower / Cabinet / Table / Oven   (Found In Kitchens)

- appearance of common objects (i.e., color; objects in pairs; objects with stripes vs. spots; object's shape)
Box / Baseball / Sphere / Basketball / Globe   (Round)

- characteristics of common objects (i.e., hot, cold)
Ice / Igloo / Popsicle / Coffee / Snowman   (Cold Things)

- animal/human homes
Aquarium / Fish / Barn / Nest / Beehive   (Animal Homes)

- animal types
Leopard / Cheetah / Lion / Tiger / Monkey   (Cats)

- natural habitats
Swamp / River / Mountain / Ocean / Pond   (Water)

- food types
Cake / Bread / Donut / Syrup / Cookie   (Baked Foods)

- food growing location (i.e., on a tree, under the ground as a root, or on a vine)
Melon / Potato / Carrot / Onion / Radish   (Root Vegetables)

- professions, community helpers
Doctor / Teacher / Wizard / Fireman / Vet   (Community Helpers)

- clothing (i.e., in what weather it's worn; on what body part it's worn)
Crown / Cowboy Hat / Cap / Gloves / Helmet   (Worn On Head)

- transportation (i.e., where things travel, land/water/air; do they have wheels?)
Cruise Ship / Canoe / Car / Yacht / Kayak   (Travel On Water)

8. Letter Matrix / Word Matrix

Directions: Look at what is in the box. You will see either words or simply letters. They go together in a certain way. Then, look at the answer choices. What answer choice would go where the question mark is?

ee	tr	tree
ll	ca	?

A. call   B. cart   C. trace   D. eel

Here, take the 2 letters in the second set of letters "tr" and put them in front of the 2 letters in the first set "ee": tr + ee = tree. With the bottom row, ca + ll = call, choice A.

Note that some questions will have words (not letters). An example in Practice Test 1 includes words, for your reference.

NON-VERBAL SECTION

9. FIGURE ANALOGIES

Directions: The pictures inside the top boxes go together in a certain way. Which answer choice goes with the picture in the bottom box like the pictures in the top boxes do? (The word "picture" here refers to a "figure" that can consist of shapes, lines, etc.)

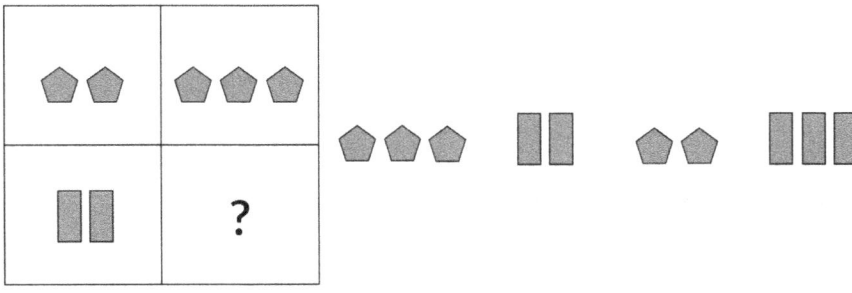

Explanation Come up with a "rule" describing how the top set is related. This shows how the left box "changes" into the right box. On the left are 2 pentagons. On the right are 3 pentagons. The rule/change is that one more of the same kind of shape was added. On the bottom are 2 rectangles. The first choice is incorrect because it shows 3 pentagons - not the same shapes as the bottom box. The second choice is incorrect - it only shows 2 rectangles. The third choice is incorrect - it has 2 pentagons. The last choice is correct - there are 3 rectangles (1 more of the same shapes that were in the left box).

Here is a list of <u>basic</u> Figure Analogy "changes."

1. Color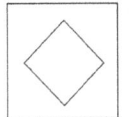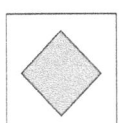

2. Size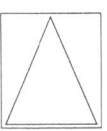

3. Amount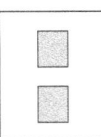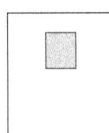

4. Color Reversal

5. Whole to Part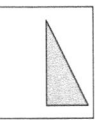

6. Shape Sides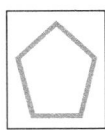

7. Rotation: 90° clockwise

8. Rotation: 90° counter-clockwise

9. Line Direction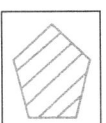

10. Flip/ Mirror Image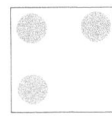

11. Two Changes: Rotation & Quantity

12. Two Changes: Rotation & Color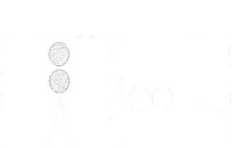

10. FIGURE CLASSIFICATION

Directions: Look at this row of pictures. These pictures are alike in some way, except for one picture. Which picture does not belong?

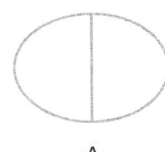 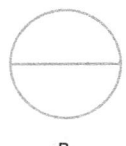  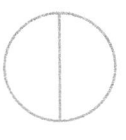 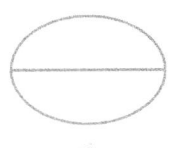

A   B   C   D   E

Try to come up with a "rule" describing how the figures in the row are alike, except for one. Here are 5 figures. They are all rounded, except for the middle shape, which is a square (not a circle or an oval). Choice C is the answer.

On the next page is a list of basic characteristics to analyze in Figure Classification questions.

Here's a list of common elements to analyze in Figure Classification questions.

How many sides do the shapes have? (Four sides)	
How are the shapes divided? (4 parts - 1 part is dark.)	
What kind of pattern / color do the shapes have? (Vertical lines)	
What direction do the shapes face? (Triangles point down)	
Does the shape have any corners? (Here, no.)	
How many shapes are in the group? (3)	
Is there a set order to the group? (Here, it's square-diamond-oval.)	

11. PATTERN MATRICES

Directions: Look at the pictures inside the boxes. They make a pattern. Look at the last box. It is empty. Look next to the boxes at the row of pictures. Which one should go inside the empty box in the bottom row?

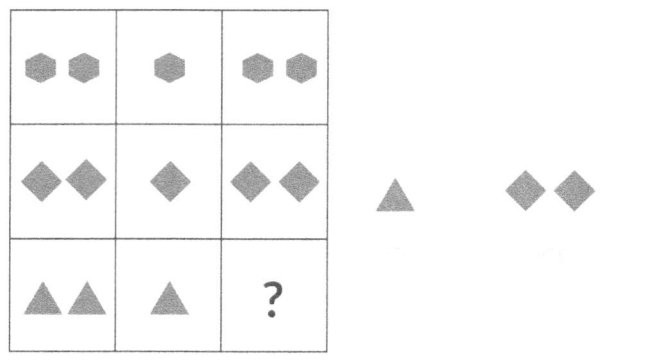

Explanation Across the top row, here is the pattern: 2 shapes - 1 shape - 2 shapes (the same kind of shape). The middle row has this pattern also. In the bottom row, we see 2 shapes - 1 shape - and... what would be the answer? It would be 2 shapes of the same kind of shape (triangles). The answer is D.

Common logic themes found in Figure Analogies are also found in Pattern Matrices.

12. FIGURE SERIES

Directions: In this row of boxes, the pictures belong together in some way. Another picture should go inside the empty box. Which picture in the row of answer choices should go in this empty box?

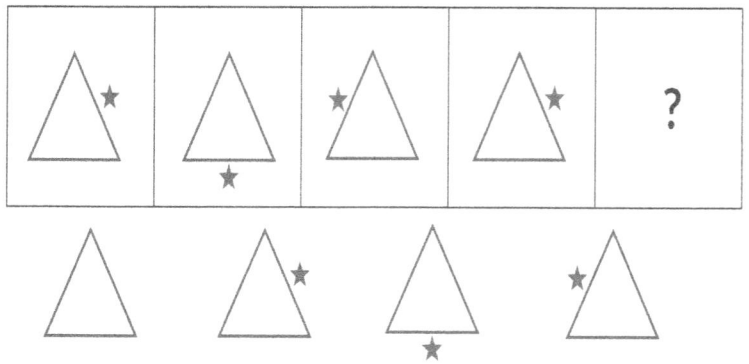

Explanation Here, figure out the pattern inside the boxes. First, the star is on the right side of the triangle, then it moves to the bottom of the triangle, then to the left side, and then to the right side. Where would the star move next? It would move to the bottom, Choice C. (The star moves clockwise around the triangle's sides.)

Common logic found in Figure Analogies is also found in Figure Series questions.

QUANTITATIVE SECTION

13. NUMBER MATRIX

Directions: Look at the numbers inside the boxes. They go together in a certain way. Which answer choice would go inside the empty box in the bottom row?

2	3	4
7	8	9
12	13	?

Here, try to come up with a "rule" that applies to the numbers going across the rows. There is also a "rule" that applies going down the columns.

Going across you see the rows, you see that the "rule" is "add 1." Going down the columns, you see that the "rule" is "add 5."

A 14   B 15   C 18   D 11

Given this, the answer is A.

14. NUMBER INFERENCES

Directions: Look at the first two sets of numbers. Come up with a rule that both of these sets follow. Take this rule to figure out which answer choice goes in the place of the question mark.

[10 →5]   [8 →4]   [14 →?]   A.2   B.7   C.28   D.16   E.1

Come up with a rule to explain how the first number "changes" into the second. It could use addition, subtraction, multiplication, or division. Write the rule by each pair. Make sure it works with both pairs. The rule is "÷ by 2", so 7 is the answer.

15. NUMBER SERIES

Directions: Which answer choice would continue the pattern?

15   13   11   9   7   ?   A.1   B.3   C.5   D.6   E.4

The numbers have made a pattern. To help figure out the pattern, write the difference between each number and the next. In this basic example, the pattern is: -2.

In easier questions, the difference between all consecutive numbers is the same (i.e., the difference between 15 & 13 = 2 and between 13 & 11 = 2). However, sometimes the difference will not continuously repeat itself, as in these examples:

9	8	6	5	3	2	?

The pattern is: -1, -2, -1, -2, etc. & the answer is 0.

1	2	4	7	11	16	?

The pattern is: +1, +2, +3, +4, etc. & the answer is 22.

4	5	9	4	5	9	?

The pattern is: 4-5-9 & the answer is 4.

0	10	0	20	0	30	?

Note: this pattern "skips." Every other number is 0. Also, every other number between a "0" has a pattern of +10 The answer is 0.

-Practice Test 1 (Workbook Format) Begins On The Next Page.-

ANTONYMS

Directions: Read the sentence and choose which word is the opposite of the word in quotation marks.

Example

The opposite of "raise" is _____.

     Ⓐ lift   Ⓑ hold   Ⓒ lower   Ⓓ increase

1   **The opposite of "gather" is _____.**

     Ⓐ collect   Ⓑ assemble   Ⓒ scatter   Ⓓ damage

2   **The opposite of "expand" is _____.**

     Ⓐ pause   Ⓑ shrink   Ⓒ enlarge   Ⓓ remain

3   **The opposite of "victory" is _____.**

     Ⓐ defeat   Ⓑ success   Ⓒ tie   Ⓓ finish

4   **The opposite of "temporary" is _____.**

     Ⓐ brief   Ⓑ rapid   Ⓒ reduce   Ⓓ permanent

Example Answer: C (The answers for the rest are in the Answer Key.)

SENTENCE COMPLETION

Directions: Read the sentence. There is a missing word. Next, look at the row of answer choices below the sentence. Which word would go best in the sentence?

Example

Alex hid his candy under his bed so that nobody would ____ it.

A miss   B hide   C cover   D discover

5   **The ____ wind howled through the night, shaking windows and tearing down trees.**

A peaceful   B powerful   C mild   D new

6   **Following the ____ swim, Alex was exhausted.**

A relaxing   B demanding   C easy   D entertaining

7   **Last month's full moon was ____ - the largest I had ever seen.**

A distant   B narrow   C secure   D immense

8   **The zookeeper's ____ helped the injured lion recover and return to its ____ in the wild.**

A kindness, cage   B patience, habitat   C mistake, family   D animals, owner

Example Answer: D (The answers for the rest are in the Answer Key.)

SENTENCE ARRANGEMENT

Note: Be sure to pay attention to whether you are asked to find the <u>first</u> word of the sentence or the <u>last</u> word of the sentence.

Example

Directions: The words below need to be arranged to make the best sentence. Which letter would the <u>first</u> word of the sentence begin with? Here are the words:

from	melted	the	sun	snow	warmth	cold

A. C   B. W   C. B   D. S

---

9   The words below need to be arranged to make the best sentence. Which letter would the <u>last</u> word of the sentence begin with? Here are the words:

running	for	the	I	was	bus	late

A. R   B. W   C. B   D. L

10 The words below need to be arranged to make the best sentence.
Which letter would the <u>last</u> word of the sentence begin with?
Here are the words:

fell   rain   the   outside   window   his

A W   B O   C T   D C

11 The words below need to be arranged to make the best sentence.
Which letter would the <u>last</u> word of the sentence begin with?
Here are the words:

waited   crowd   the   patiently   for   train   the

A W   B C   C A   D T

12 The words below need to be arranged to make the best sentence.
Which letter would the <u>first</u> word of the sentence begin with?
Here are the words:

carried   wind   leaves   across   fallen   field   a

A W   B F   C B   D A

ARITHMETIC REASONING

Note: The primary skill tested here is <u>not</u> your child's math level. You'll find some questions use quite basic math operations. The primary skill tested here involves taking the words in the math problem, turning the words into the correct math equations, and solving the equations.

Directions: Read the question then choose your answer.

Example 1

Mark and Ana sold boxes of cookies to raise money for their school. Ana sold twelve boxes. Mark sold five less boxes than Ana. How many boxes did Mark sell?

A 7   B 5   C 12   D 27

Example 2

Leo collects model cars. He had ten cars. Then, he gave away all of them except six cars to his cousin. How many cars does Leo have left?

A 10   B 6   C 5   D 4

13   Two teams were competing in a relay: Maria and Jason were racing against Tony and Sarah. Maria ran fourteen laps, Jason ran twenty-eight laps, Tony ran twenty laps, and Sarah ran thirteen laps. How many laps did Maria's team run in total?

A 14   B 32   C 75   D 42

14   During a baking contest, Sophie made 3 pies, Lily made 2 cakes, Jason made a pie for himself, Matt made 4 cupcakes, and Alex made 2 pies. How many pies were made in all?

A 4   B 5   C 6   D 12

15   Ellie had twelve balloons. She gave five of them to Sarah and the rest to Jamie. Jamie then gave two of her balloons to Sarah. How many balloons does Sarah have now?

A 5   B 7   C 9   D 12

16   There are eight pencils in each box. If you bought four boxes, how many pencils would you have in total?

A 32   B 24   C 16   D 12

LOGICAL SELECTION

Directions: Read the sentence and choose which word best completes the sentence.

Tip: Be sure to think carefully about whether or not each answer choice is truly needed.

Example

A book must have _____.

A pictures   B an index   C images   D a price   E pages

17   **A car must have _____.**

A a radio   B a steering wheel   C heat   D air conditioning

18   **A chair must always have _____.**

A a cushion   B a backrest   C arms   D legs

19   **A mountain must always have _____.**

A a peak   B snow   C trees   D rocks

20   **A road must always have _____.**

A an end   B signs   C lanes   D pavement

VERBAL ANALOGIES

Directions: The first set of words goes together in a certain way. Look at the second set of words. The answer is missing. Which answer choice would make the second set go together in the same way that the first set goes together?

Tip: Think of a "rule" or a sentence describing how each pair goes together.

Example

read → book : listen →

A ears   B volume   C magazine   D loud   E radio

21   **pull → push : north →   ?**

    A down   B south   C northern   D east

22   **hair → fur : foot →   ?**

    A hand   B claw   C animal   D paw

23   **house → attic : mountain →   ?**

    A hike   B snow   C peak   D trail

24   **weight → pound : temperature →   ?**

    A heat   B degree   C number   D thermometer

Example Answer: E You read a book. You listen to a radio. (The first word is the verb that goes with the second.)

VERBAL CLASSIFICATION

Directions: Which word does not go with the others?

Tips: Figure out how all of the words, except for one, are alike.

Try to come up with a "rule" describing this. Then, take this "rule," and figure out which of the answer choices does not follow it.

If you find that more than one choice does not follow the rule, then try to come up with a rule that is more specific.

The "rule" in the example is: types of instruments.

In the example, "concert" *has to do with* the rule (instruments), but it is not a *type* of instrument.

Example

1   **Which word does not go with the others?**

(A) piano   (B) drums   (C) trumpet   (D) concert   (E) violin

25 **Which word does not go with the others?**

A purple   B color   C blue   D red   E black

26 **Which word does not go with the others?**

A glad   B joyful   C delighted   D cheerful   E smile

27 **Which word does not go with the others?**

A skis   B dice   C gloves   D fruit   E socks

28 **Which word does not go with the others?**

A calculator   B sundial   C hourglass   D stopwatch   E clock

LETTER MATRIX / WORD MATRIX

Directions: Look at what is in the box. You will see either words or simply letters. They go together in a certain way. Then, look at the answer choices. What answer choice would go where the question mark is?

Tips: First, figure out if the things in the boxes are words or simply letters.

Then, see if you can figure out how they go together. First, look across. Example 1 is like this. You must take the 2 letters in the second set of letters "da" and put them in front of the 2 letters in the first set "te": da + te = date

If you cannot see how they go together by going across from left to right, then, starting from the first column, look up and down. Example 2 is like this. Going from the top word to the bottom word, you see that the words are in alphabetical order. This "rule" applies for all the words: ant > box > cat > dog > egg.

EXAMPLE 1

te	da	date
ok	to	?

A tea   B took   C tote   D ok

EXAMPLE 2

ant	cat	egg
box	dog	?

A fruit   B exit   C all   D yolk

29

de	dr	deer
lo	lk	?

A lord   B led   C look   D leer

30

en	ov	oven
al	me	?

A move   B lame   C oval   D meal

31

between	dense	follow
cold	early	?

A giggle   B future   C late   D mist

32

wide	create	shout
narrow	destroy	?

A yell   B whisper   C damage   D announce

FIGURE CLASSIFICATION

Directions: Which choice does not go with the others?

Tips: Figure out how all of the choices, except for one, are alike.

Try to come up with a "rule" describing this. Then, take this "rule," and figure out which of the answer choices does not follow it.

If you find that more than one choice does not follow the rule, then try to come up with a rule that is more specific.

The "rule" in example is: the arrow points to the left.

Common rules for figure classification involve:

- direction that the shapes point
- direction that the lines point
- types of lines inside the shape
- color of the shapes / color of the lines
- number (quantity) of shapes in each group
- types of shapes in each group
- number of sides the shapes have

1

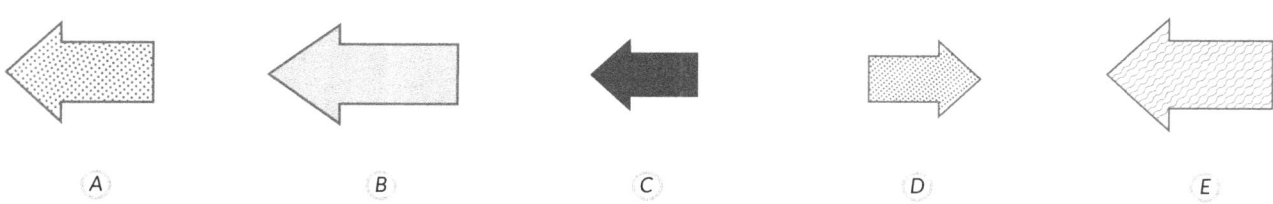

A   B   C   D   E

33

A B C D E

34

A B C D E

35

A B C D E

36

A B C D E

FIGURE ANALOGIES

Directions: Look at the top boxes. The pictures inside belong together in a certain way. Look at the bottom boxes. One is empty. Which answer choice would go with the picture in the bottom box in the same way that the top boxes go together?

Tips: Use the same methodology to complete Figure Analogies as you used for Verbal Analogies.

Work through these together so your child sees how the first set is related.

Together, come up with a "rule" to describe how the first set is related. Then, in the second set, look at the first picture. Take this "rule," use it together with the first picture, and figure out which of the answer choices would follow that same rule.

For answer choices that do not follow this rule, eliminate them. If your child finds that more than one choice follows this rule, then try to come up with a rule that is more specific.

In the example, we see that the smaller middle shape from the first box on the left gets bigger and is alone in the box on the right.

EXAMPLE

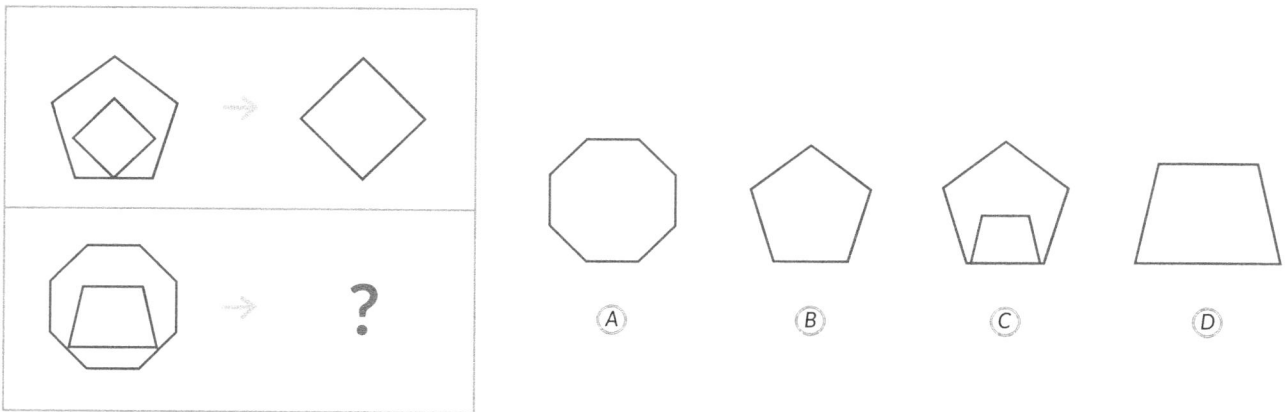

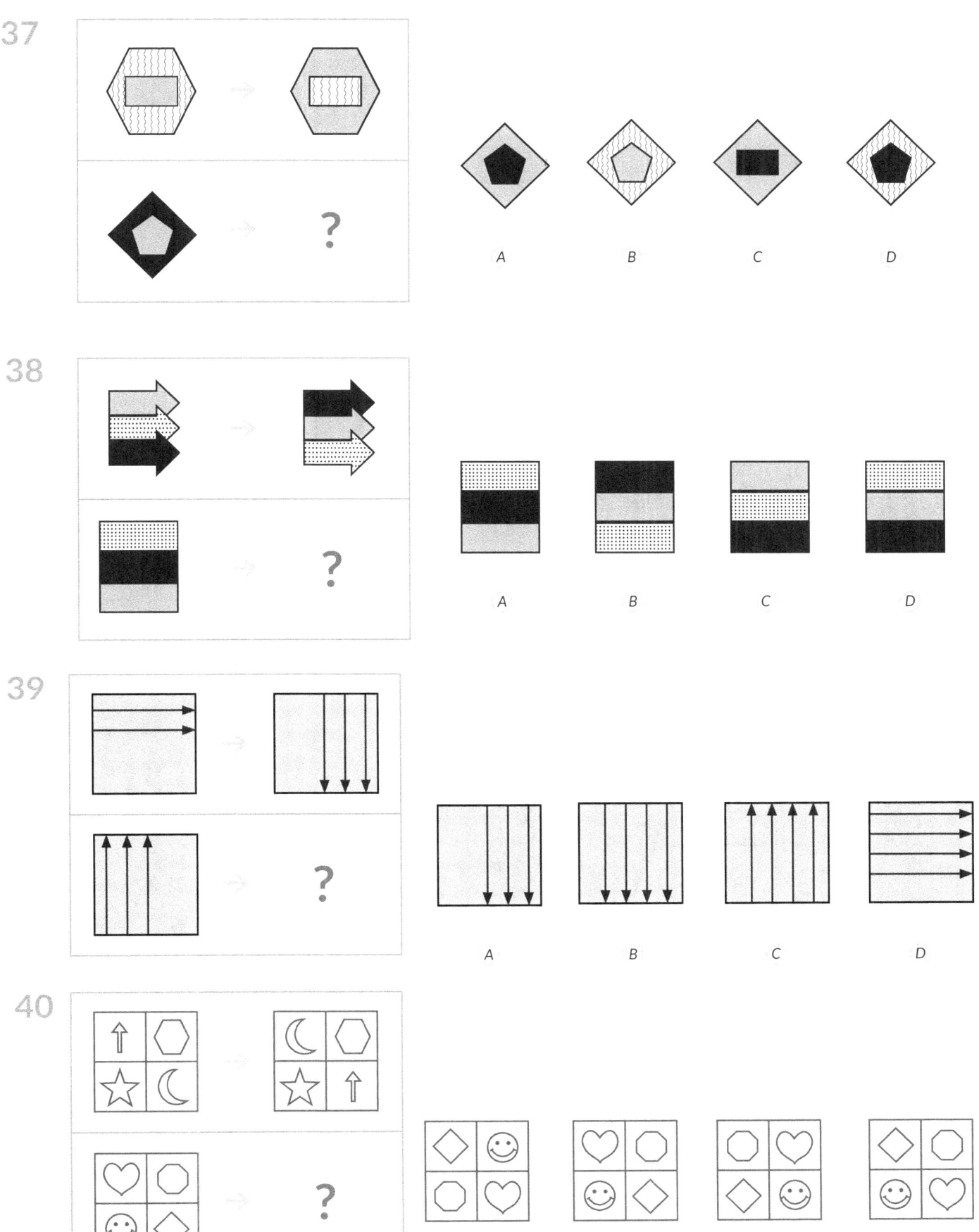

37

38

39

40

A B C D

FIGURE SERIES

Directions: The pictures inside the boxes go together in a certain way. Another picture should go inside the empty box. Under the boxes is a row of pictures. Which one should go in this empty box?

Tips: See if you can spot the pattern that the design in each box has made, as you go from left to right.

The last box must continue this pattern.

In the example below, there is an arrow. First, look at how the arrow changes position (how the arrow rotates). It rotates 90 degrees clockwise. Look at the last box. When the gray arrow that is pointed left rotates 90 degrees, it will face up.

Next, look at how the design inside the arrow changes. First, it is gray, then filled with dots, then filled with wavy lines, and finally it is gray again. If you look at the beginning of the pattern, you see that after an arrow is filled with gray, next it is filled with dots.

EXAMPLE

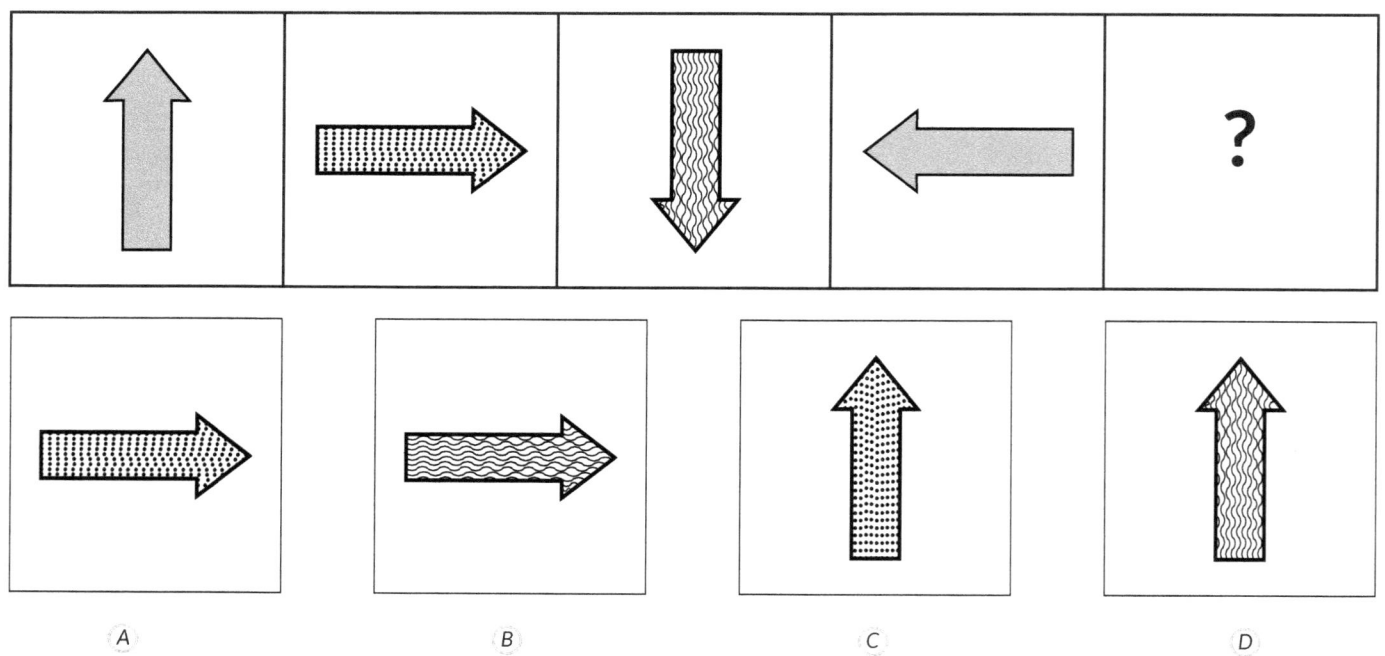

41

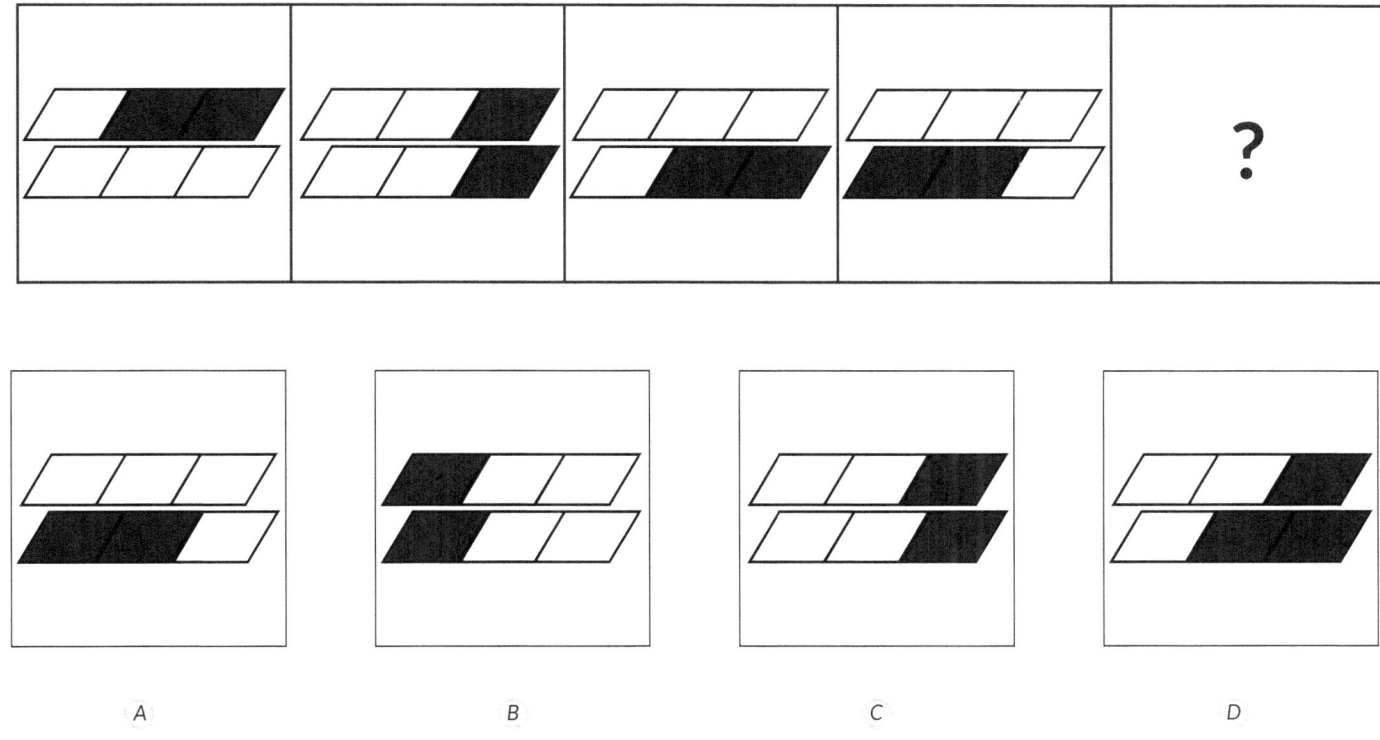

42

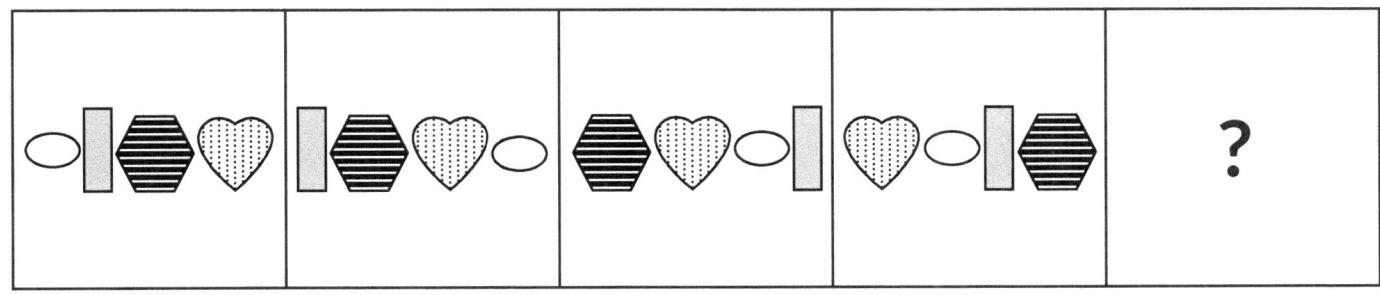

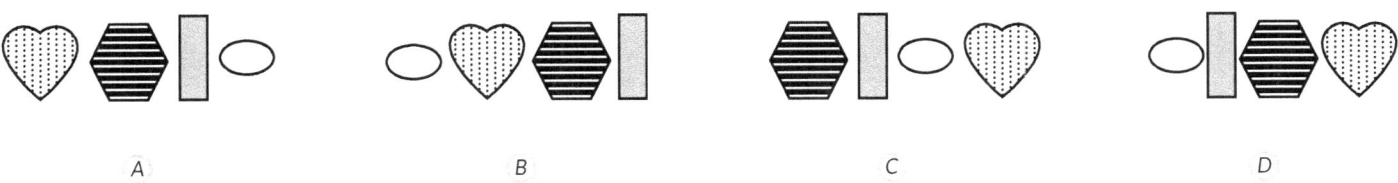

PATTERN MATRIX

Directions: Look at the pictures inside the boxes. They go together in a certain way. Which answer choice would go inside the empty box in the bottom row?

Tips: See if you can spot the pattern that the design in each box has made, as you go from left to right.

There may also be a pattern that goes up and down.

The last box must continue this pattern.

In the example below, going across the first row, we see that there are five wavy lines. There are 4 gray lines and 1 black line. As you go across, from left to right, we see that the black line moves down one. This also happens in the middle row. This also happens in the last row.

There's also a pattern going down the columns, but it is a different pattern. There are gray lines and black lines. However, the black line stays in the same position, and the number of gray lines decreases by 1 line.

EXAMPLE

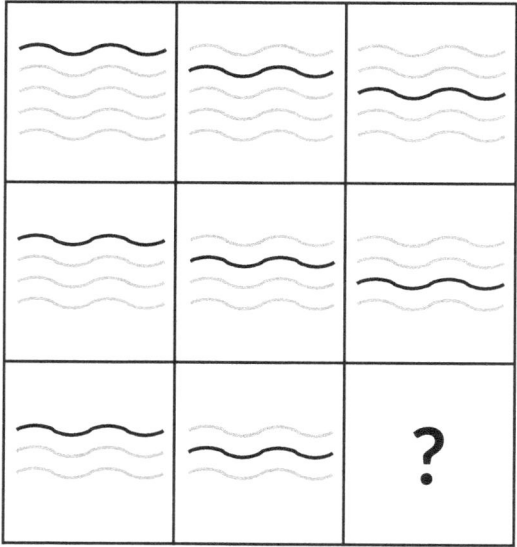

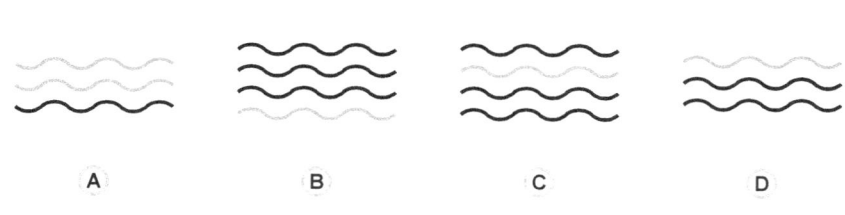

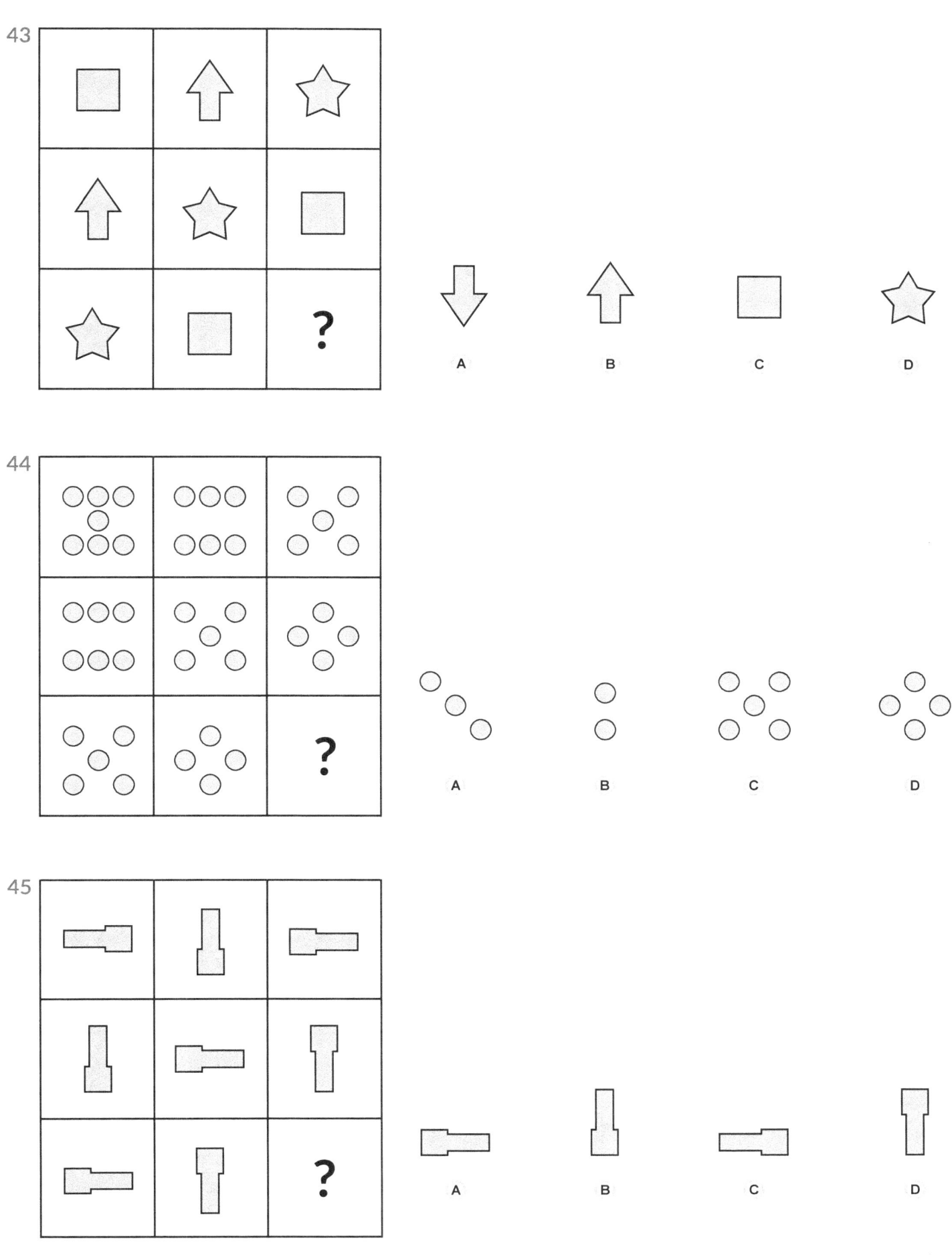

NUMERIC MATRIX

Directions: Look at the numbers inside the boxes. They go together in a certain way. Which answer choice would go inside the empty space in the bottom row?

Tips: See if you can spot the pattern that the design in each box has made, as you go from left to right.

There is also a pattern that goes up and down.

The last box must continue this pattern.

In the example, going across the first row, we see that the pattern is "subtract 5": 13 - 5 = 8; 8 - 5 = 3; 15 - 5 = 10; 10 - 5 = 5; 17 - 5 = 12; 12 - 5 = ?

Going down the columns, we see that the pattern is "add 2": 13 + 2 = 15; 15 + 2 = 17; 8 + 2 = 10; 10 + 2 = 12; 3 + 2 = 5; 5 + 2 = ?

Note: The pattern may change as you go across rows. For example, in #47, going across the rows, you first subtract 9, then you add 3: 29 - 9 = 20; 20 + 3 = 23.

EXAMPLE

13	8	3
15	10	5
17	12	?

(A) 6   (B) 5   (C) 14   (D) 7

46

34	52	70
22	40	58
10	28	?

A 40   B 12   C 56   D 46

47

| 29 | 20 | 23 |
| ? | 30 | 33 |

A 39   B 33   C 20   D 32

48

| 18 | 27 | 30 |
| ? | 39 | 42 |

A 32   B 30   C 39   D 40

49

48	40	55
37	29	44
26	18	?

A 7   B 22   C 23   D 33

NUMERIC INFERENCES

Directions: Look at the first two sets of numbers. The numbers in each set belong together in a certain way. Look at the last set. A number is missing. Which answer choice would go with the number(s) in the last set in the same way that the first two sets go together?

Tips: Use the same methodology to complete Number Inferences as you used for Figure Analogies and Verbal Analogies.

Work through these together so your child sees how the first two sets are related.

Together, come up with a "rule" to describe how they are related. Take this "rule," use it together with the missing number in the last set, and figure out which of the answer choices would follow that same rule.

In the example, look at the first set. How would you go from 3 to 6? Try to come up with a rule. You could try the rule "add 3." However, this does not work with the second set because 4 + 3 does not equal 8. It must be a different rule. How else can you go from 3 to 6? You can "multiply by 2." Let's try this rule. This rule also works in the second set: 4 x 2 = 8. So, what does 5 x 2 equal?

Note: The rule can also involve two operations. For example, in #53, in each group of 3 numbers, the first number is multiplied by 2, then this answer is added to 2.

EXAMPLE

2   [3 → 6]   [4 → 8]   [5 → ?]

    A 2   B 5   C 10   D 25   E 12

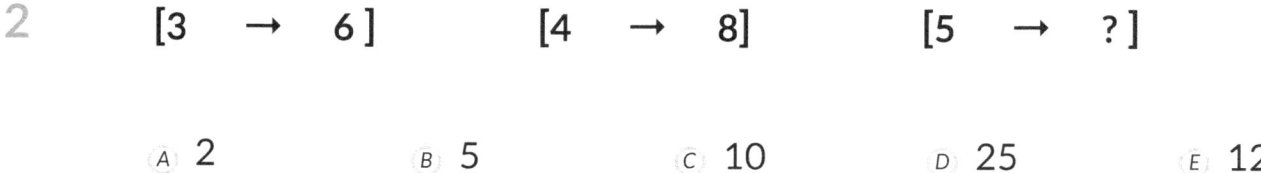

Example Answer: C (See explanation above.)

50   [10 → 5]   [18 → 9]   [14 → ?]

    A 2   B 12   C 16   D 14   E 7

51   [37 → 29]   [47 → 39]   [52 → ?]

    A 60   B 40   C 59   D 44   E 50

52   [2,653 → 6]   [4,857 → 8]   [5,021 → ?]

    A 9   B 5   C 0   D 1   E 2

53   [3, 6, 8]   [5, 10, 12]   [?, 12, 14]

    A 4   B 5   C 6   D 7   E 2

NUMERIC SERIES

Directions: Which answer choice would complete the pattern?

Tips: Here, you must figure out a pattern that the numbers have made.

It could involve adding, subtracting, multiplying, or dividing. It could change from one number to the next.

In between each set of numbers, try figure out what has changed and write it in between the two numbers.

Look at the example below.

How would you go from 23 to 26? You would add 3. How would you go from 26 to 29? You would add 3. Let's see if this pattern continues. Going from 29 to 32, then from 32 to 35, and finally from 35 to 38, we see that it does. The pattern is "add 3."

Note: Some questions may have a pattern that appears to "skip" numbers. For example, #56, you see that every other number is 0. What pattern can you see that the other numbers have made (the 12, 13, 14, etc.)?

| 23 | 26 | 29 | 32 | 35 | 38 | ? |

A 43   B 42   C 41   D 45   E 37

54 5 6 8 9 11 12 ?

A 10 B 17 C 15 D 14 E 13

55 5 7 10 12 15 17 ?

A 19 B 18 C 24 D 20 E 22

56 0 12 0 13 0 14 ?

A 15 B 14 C 0 D 1 E 16

57 39 37 38 36 37 35 ?

A 36 B 37 C 35 D 34 E 30

- Practice Test 2 Begins On The Next Page -

*Note: Questions in Practice Test 2 & 3 are <u>not</u> grouped by question type (unlike Practice Test 1). When your child takes the actual test, questions will most likely not be grouped by question type.

PRACTICE TEST 2

1   **The opposite of decrease is _____.**

    Ⓐ reduce   Ⓑ drop   Ⓒ continue   Ⓓ increase

---

2   **The words below must be arranged to make the best sentence. Which letter would the first word of the sentence begin with? Here are the words:**

    finished   the   a   runners   exhausted   marathon

    Ⓐ T   Ⓑ A   Ⓒ R   Ⓓ M

---

3   **Ben has 20 marbles. He gave away all of the marbles except 8 marbles. How many marbles does Ben have left?**

    Ⓐ 12   Ⓑ 10   Ⓒ 8   Ⓓ 6

---

4   **Which choice makes the second set of pictures go together in the same way as the first set?**

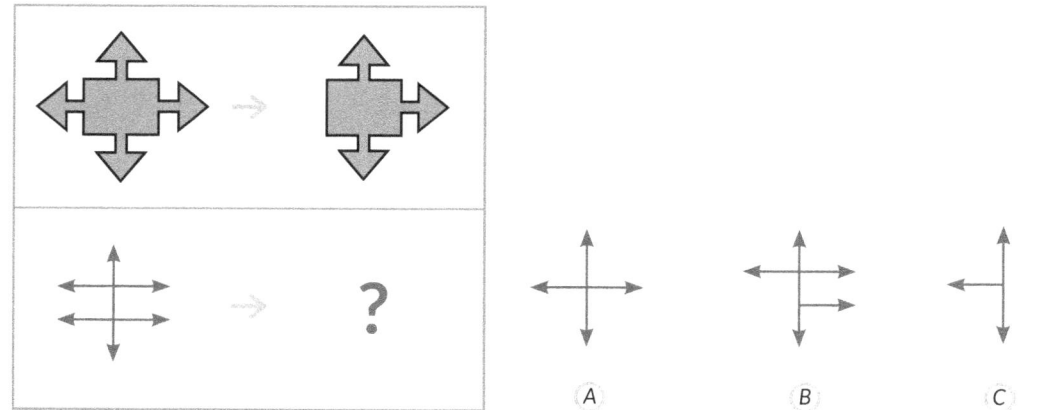

5 The opposite of frequent is _____.

    A rare   *B* constant   *C* regular   *D* often

6 An airplane must have _____.

    A seats   *B* a bathroom   *C* passengers   *D* wings

7 Which word does not go with the others?

    A saw   *B* knife   *C* lawn mower   *D* razor   *E* straw

8 Which word does not go with the others?

    A tired   *B* nap   *C* drowsy   *D* exhausted   *E* sleepy

9 Which shape group does not go with the others?

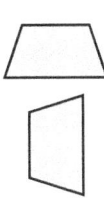  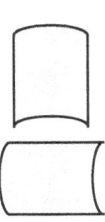 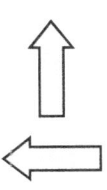 

    A   **B**   **C**   **D**   **E**

10 The words below need to be arranged to make the best sentence. Which letter would the <u>last</u> word of the sentence begin with? Here are the words:

organized   papers   students   neatly   on   a   table

(A) A   (B) T   (C) R   (D) M

---

11 A group of third graders is having a bake sale. Ms. Smith baked twelve cakes. Mr. Lee baked seven fewer cakes than Ms. Smith. How many cakes did Mr. Lee bake?

(A) 6   (B) 5   (C) 4   (D) 7

---

12 Which choice makes the second set of pictures go together in the same way as the first set?

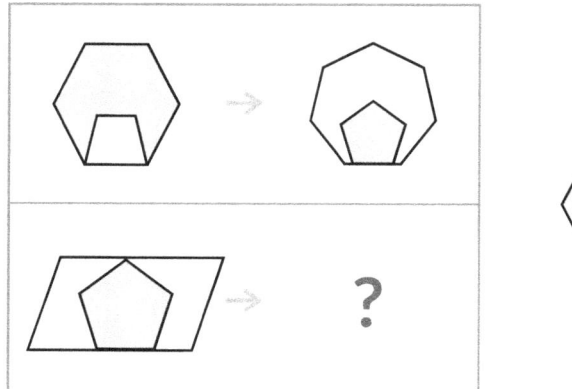

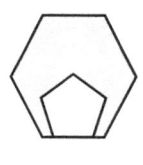 (A)   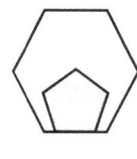 (B)    (C)    (D)

---

13 The numbers in the below box go together in a certain way. Which answer choice would replace the question mark?

43	38	33
?	43	38

(A) 39   (B) 43   (C) 48   (D) 53

14 Which answer choice best completes the sentence?

The ____ puppy explored the yard, sniffing the flowers and barking at the neighbor's cat.

A lazy   B curious   C silent   D calm

15

me	mt	meet
fo	fd	?

A food   B dome   C feet   D fold

16 Which shape does not go with the others?

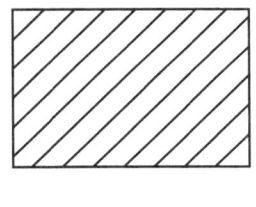 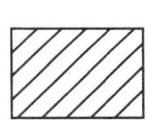 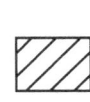  

A   B   C   D   E

17 Which answer choice best completes the sentence?

____ history museums contain art from thousands of years ago.

A Modern   B Futuristic   C Ancient   D Contemporary

18 What number should replace the question mark (?) so that all three sets of numbers go together in the same way?

[25 → 18]   [38 → 31]   [56 → ?]

A 57   B 62   C 49   D 8   E 7

19 The words below must be arranged to make the best sentence. Which letter would the **first** word of the sentence begin with? Here are the words:

mountain   climbed   steep   the   hikers   up   five   peak

A D   B H   C F   D M

20 Carlos prepared four trays of brownies. Each tray had nine brownies. How many brownies did he prepare in total?

A 13   B 32   C 5   D 36

21 A desert always has _____.

A heat   B cactus   C sun   D dryness

22 Which answer choice makes the second set of words go together in the same way that the first set does?

ruler → length : compass → ?

A maps   B direction   C trip   D thermometer

23 Which answer choice makes the second set of words go together in the same way that the first set does?

carriage → car : bicycle → ?

A wagon   B unicycle   C motorcycle   D skateboard

24 The words below need to be arranged to make the best sentence. Which letter would the <u>last</u> word of the sentence begin with? Here are the words:

reports   finished   student   his   a   and   submitted   them

A T   B I   C S   D R

25 A forest always has _____.

A hills   B trails   C trees   D wildlife

26 Which answer choice makes the second set of words go together in the same way that the first set does?

mechanic → engine : plumber →   ?

A truck   B drain   C roof   D wrench

27 Which answer choice makes the second set of words go together in the same way that the first set does?

bread → grain : paper →   ?

A tree   B book   C pencil   D sheet

28 The words in the below box go together in a certain way. Which answer choice would go in place of the question mark?

gorilla	iguana	kangaroo
horse	jackal	?

A hyena   B monkey   C koala   D lemur

29   The opposite of maximum is ____.

A greatest   B small   C minimum   D peak

---

30   Which answer choice best completes the sentence?

The soldiers fought against their ____ during the battle.

A partner   B teammate   C tank   D rival

---

31   Ben wants to buy a comic book that costs $18. He earns $9 a week by walking his neighbor's dog. How many weeks will he need to save before he can buy the book?

A 3   B 1   C 2   D 4

---

32   A volcano always has ____.

A fire   B magma   C lava   D an earthquake

---

33   The numbers below form a pattern. What number should go in place of the question mark to continue the pattern?

43   51   59   67   75   83   ?

○ 91   ○ 81   ○ 90   ○ 88   ○ 86

34 The opposite of rarely is ____.

    A often   B rarest   C seldom   D scarcely

35 Which answer choice best completes the sentence?

The view of the vast desert and deep canyons made for an incredible ____.

    A swamp   B forest   C jungle   D landscape

36 Which word does not go with the others?

    A raccoon   B rabbit   C rhinoceros   D chicken   E horse

37 Which word does not go with the others?

    A water   B sand   C gasoline   D vinegar   E milk

38 Which shape group does not go with the others?

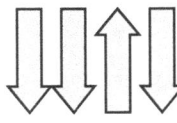 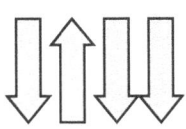 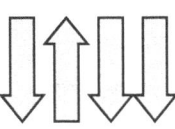 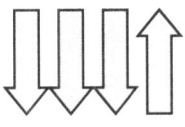 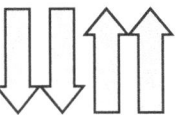

    A   B   C   D   E

39 The numbers below form a pattern. What number should go in place of the question mark to continue the pattern?

    2   4   8   16   ?

    24   22   32   20   34

40 The words in the below box go together in a certain way. Which answer choice would go in place of the question mark?

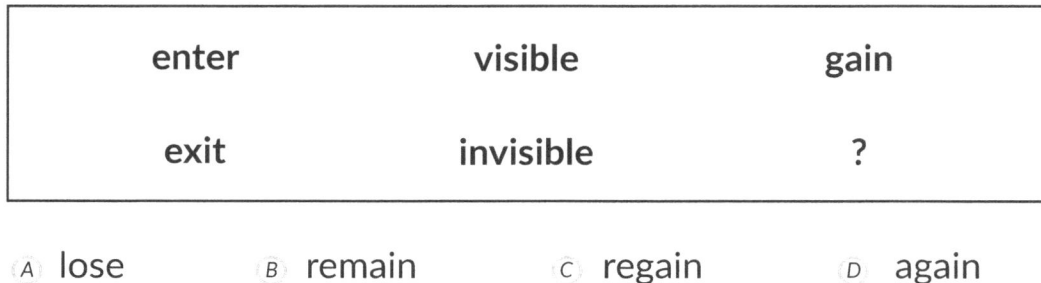

enter	visible	gain
exit	invisible	?

A lose   B remain   C regain   D again

41 Which choice makes the second set of pictures go together in the same way as the first set?

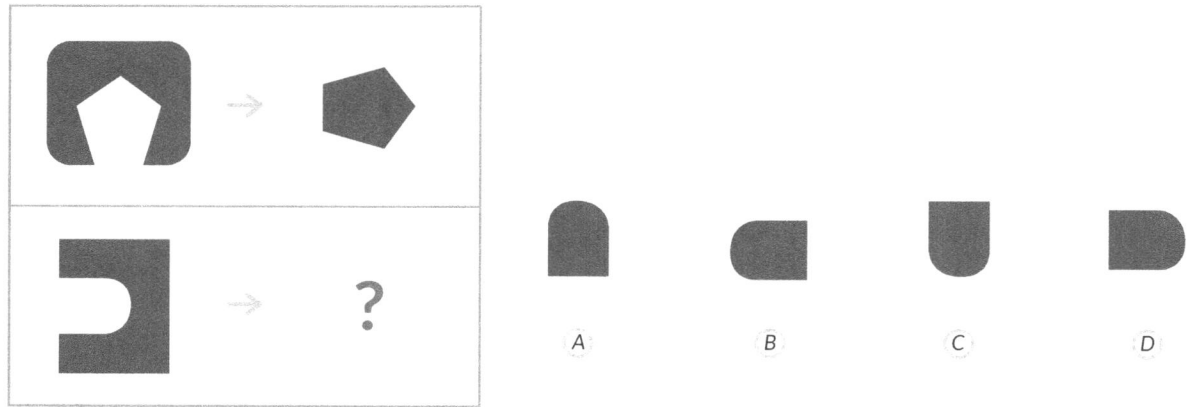

A   B   C   D

42 Which shape group does not go with the others?

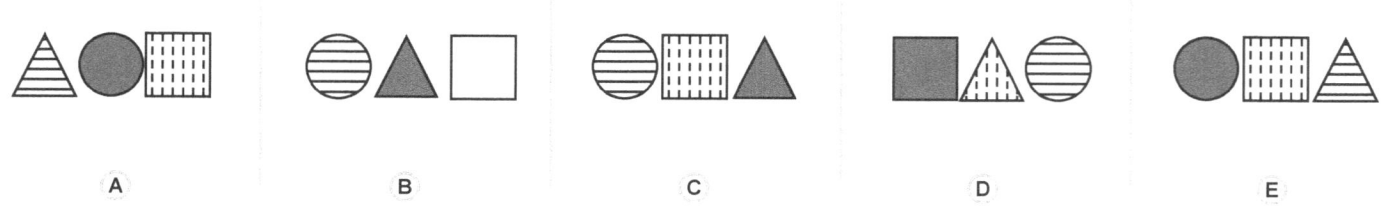

A   B   C   D   E

43 What number comes next in the series?

12   13   15   16   18   19   21   22   ?

19   26   20   24   25

44 The words in the below box go together in a certain way. Which answer choice would go in place of the question mark?

brave	create	divide
begin	calm	?

A cherish   B delicate   C effort   D subtract

45 Which choice makes the second set of pictures go together in the same way as the first set?

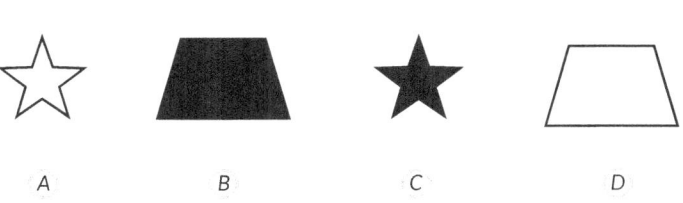

    A   B   C   D

46 What number should replace the question mark (?) so that all three sets of numbers go together in the same way?

[1,653 → 5]   [9,817 → 1]   [4,921 → ?]

A 9   B 5   C 0   D 1   E 2

47 What number comes next in the series?

40   39   37   34   30   25   19   12   ?

25   20   6   4   8

The numbers in the below box go together in a certain way. Which answer choice would replace the question mark?

49	45	41
56	52	48
63	59	?

A) 55   B) 42   C) 43   D) 65

---

49   **What comes next in the series?**

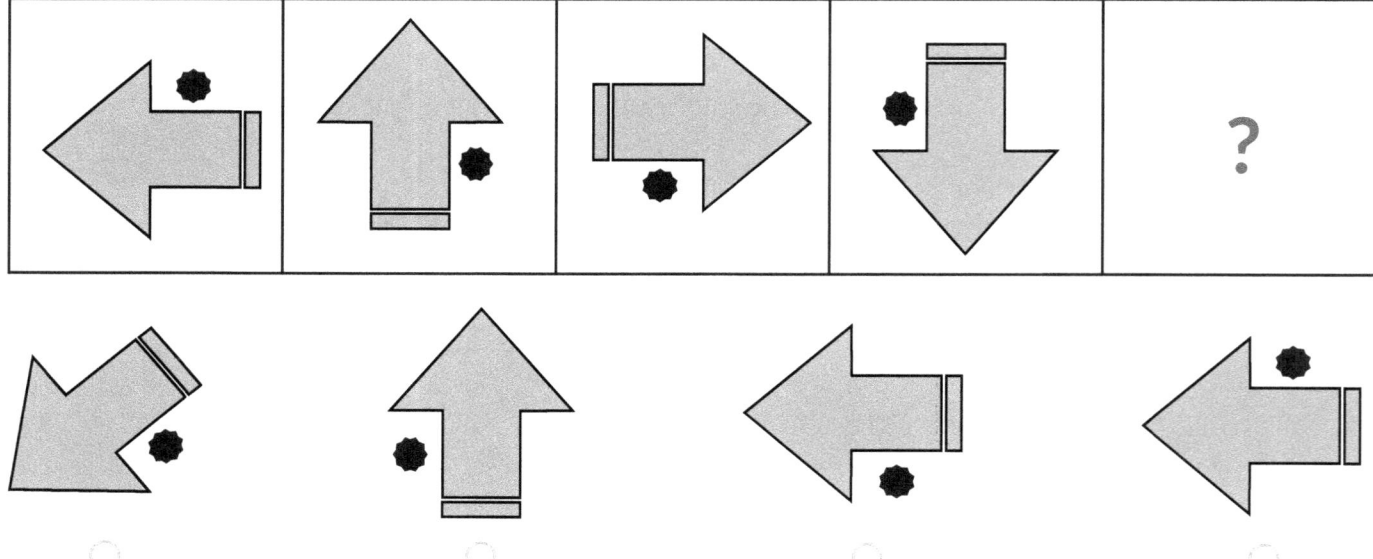

50 The numbers in the below box go together in a certain way. Which answer choice would replace the question mark?

38	49	53
?	63	67

A 59   B 52   C 42   D 62

51 What comes next in the series?

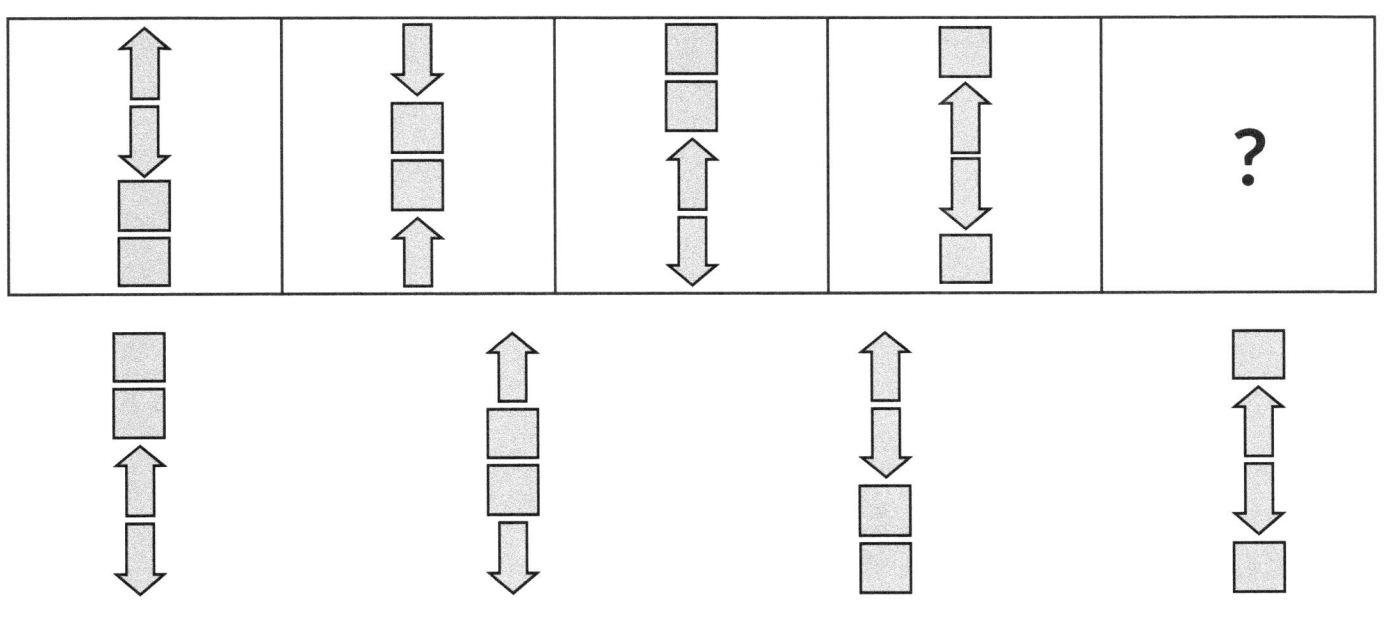

52 The numbers in the below box go together in a certain way. Which answer choice would replace the question mark?

71	80	89
?	90	99

A 99   B 80   C 89   D 81

53 **What comes next in the series?**

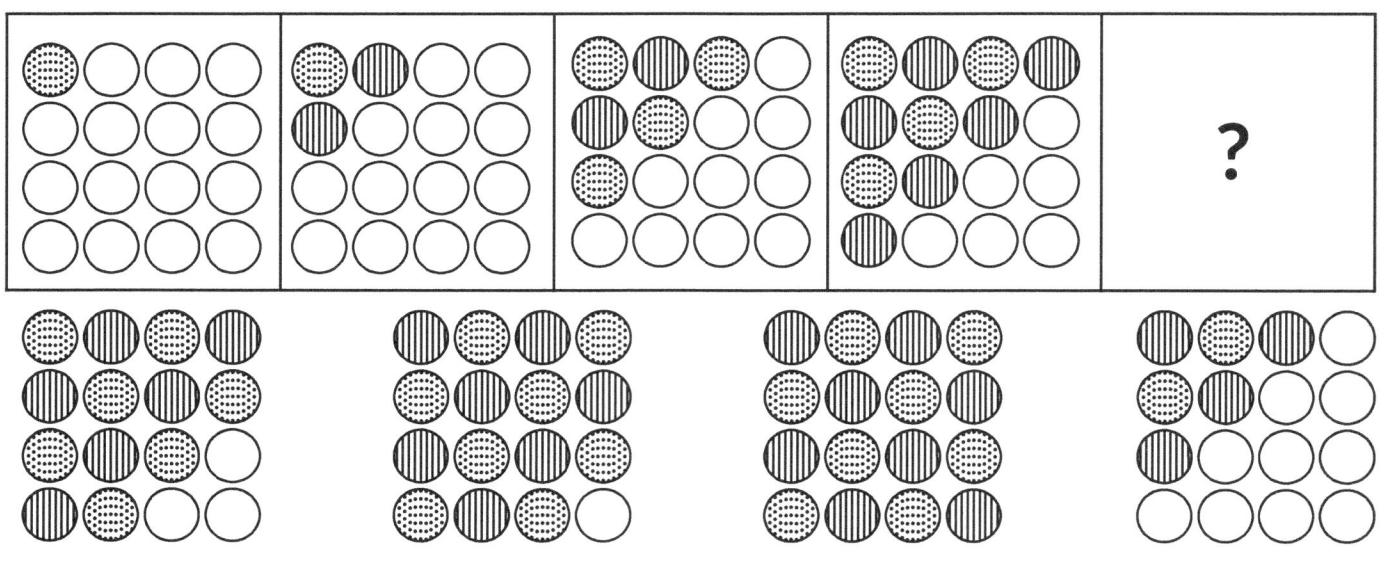

54 **The objects in the boxes go together in a certain way. What goes in the empty box?**

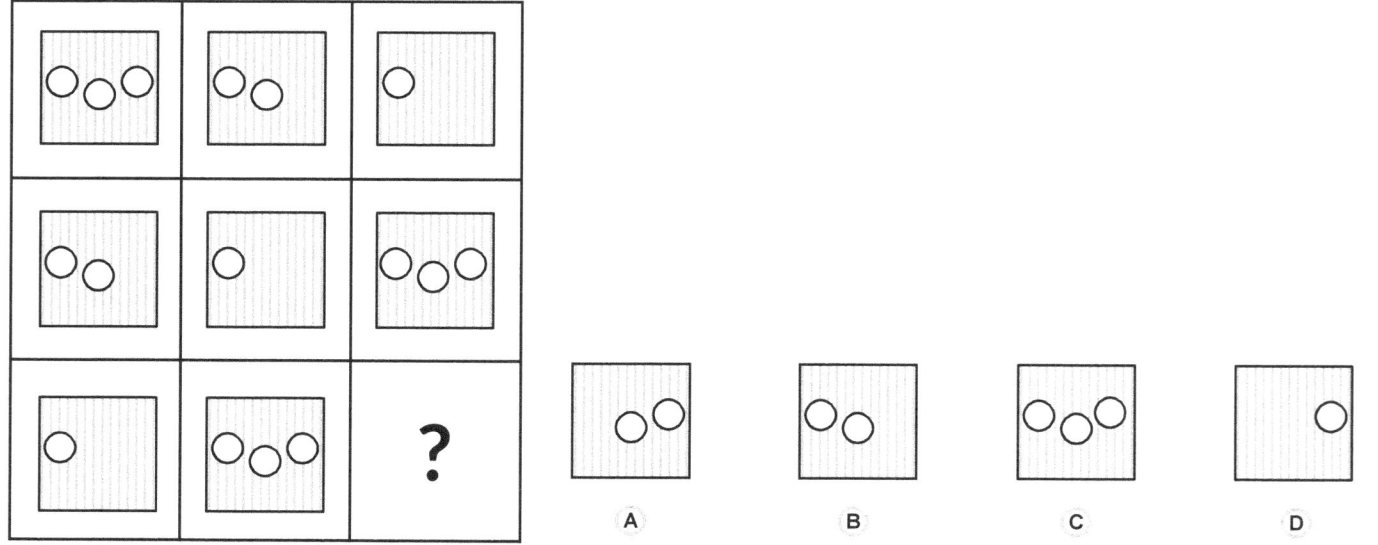

55   What comes next in the series?

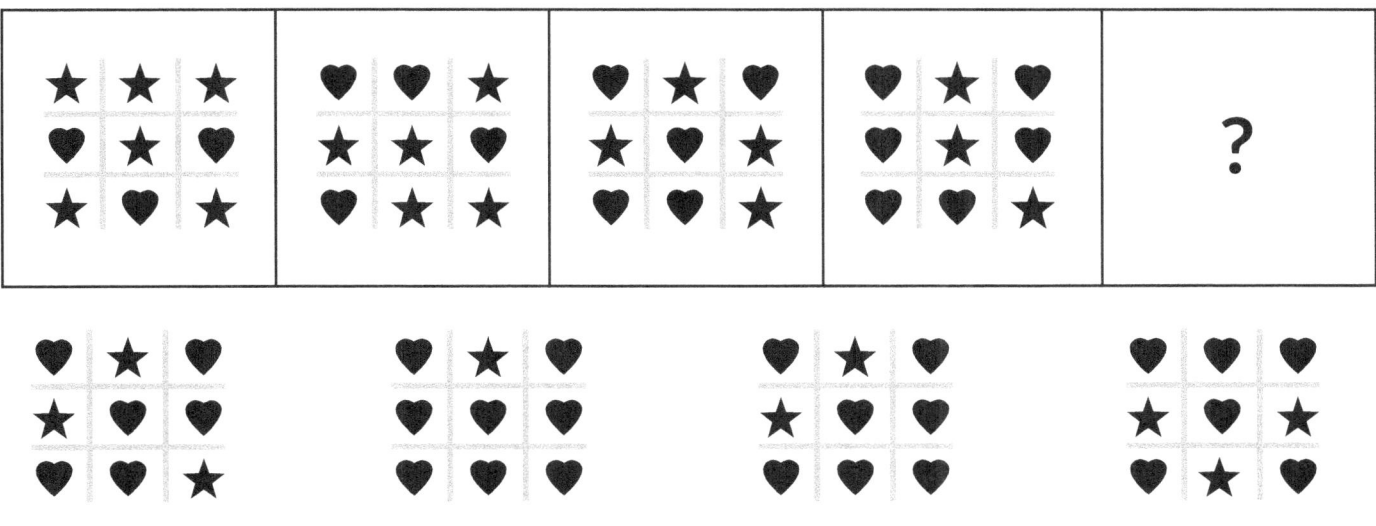

56   The objects in the boxes go together in a certain way. What goes in the empty box?

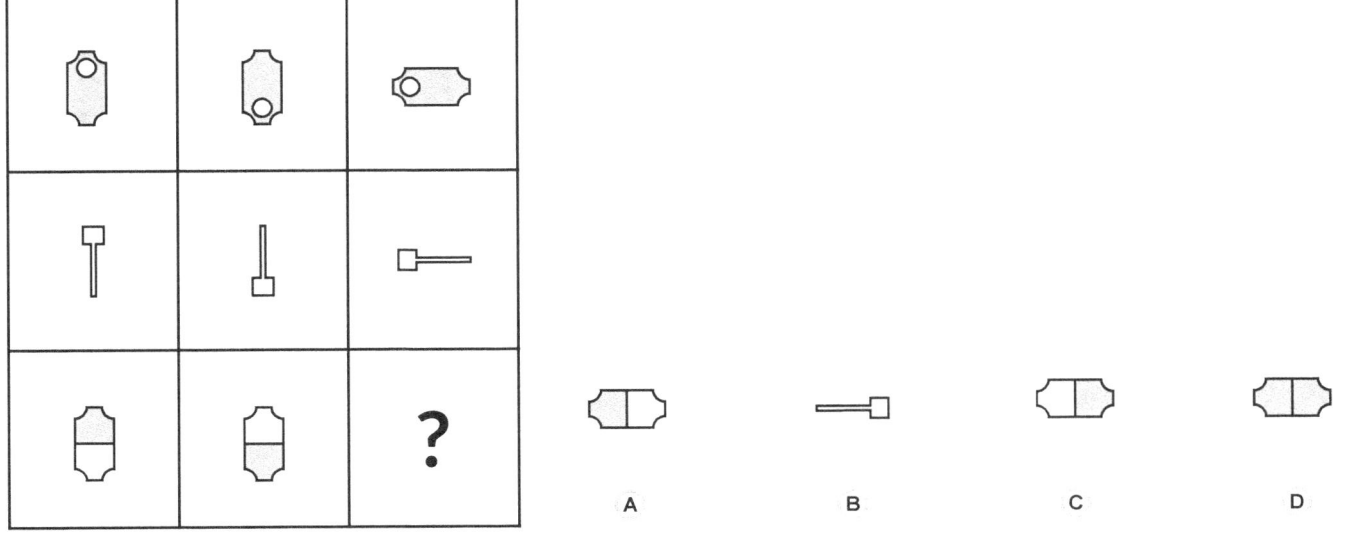

57   The objects in the boxes go together in a certain way. What goes in the empty box?

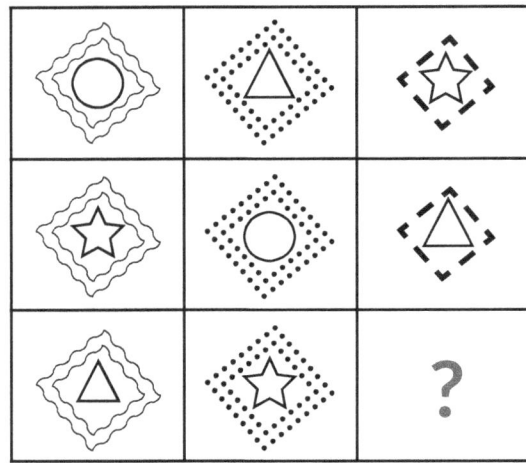    

58   What comes next in the series?

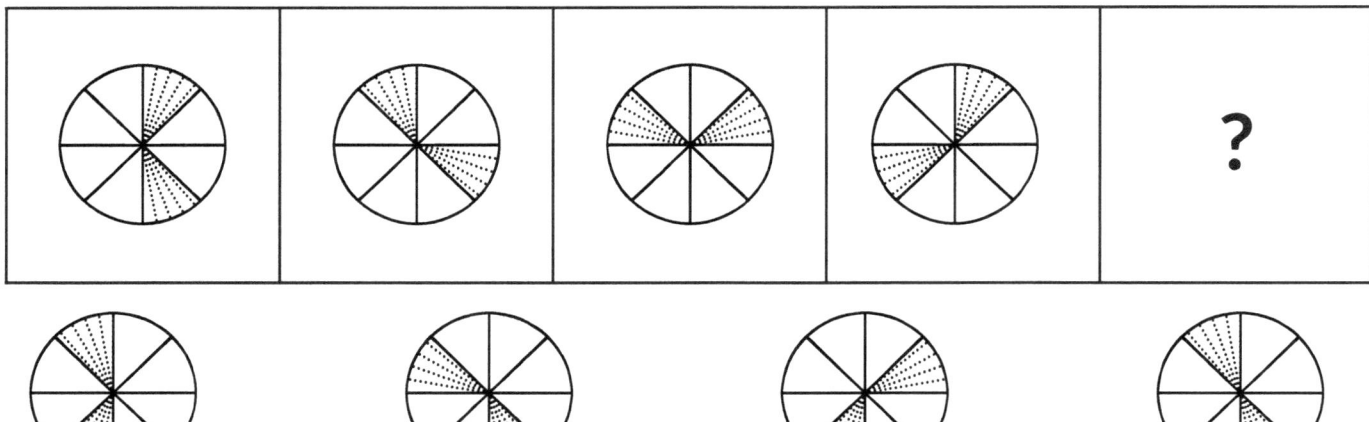

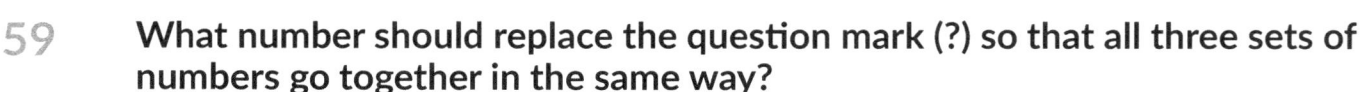

59   What number should replace the question mark (?) so that all three sets of numbers go together in the same way?

[36 → 12]   [3 → 1]   [18 → ?]

A 9   B 21   C 15   D 3   E 6

60 The objects in the boxes go together in a certain way.
What goes in the empty box?

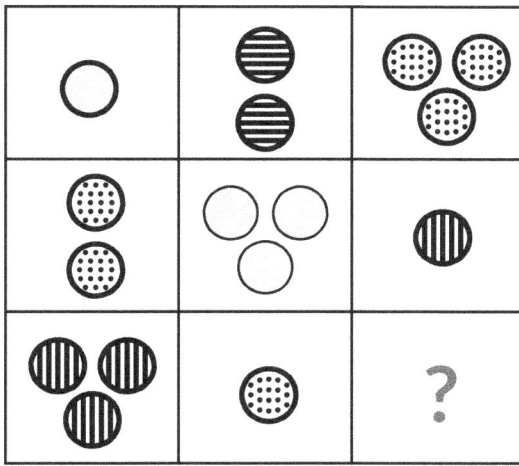    

61 The objects in the boxes go together in a certain way. What goes in the empty box?

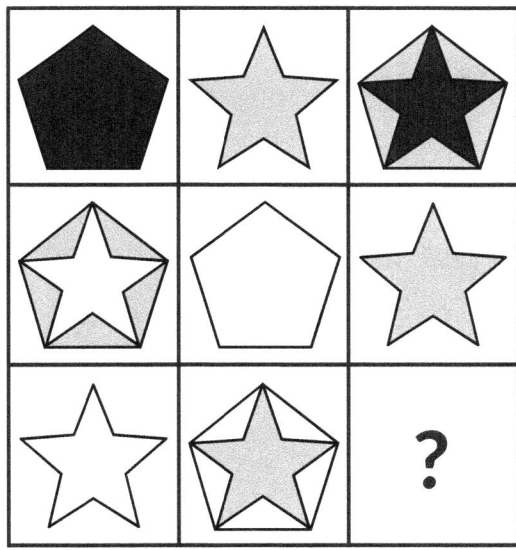  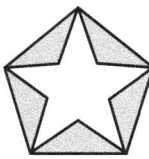  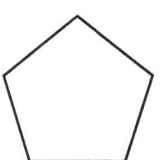

62 What number should replace the question mark (?) so that all three sets of numbers go together in the same way?

[24 → 12]   [1/2 → 1/4]   [50 → ?]

A 25   B 20   C 38   D 100   E 52

- Practice Test 3 Begins On The Next Page -

PRACTICE TEST 3

1   **The opposite of scarce is _____.**

    A limited   B abundant   C sparse   D narrow

---

2   **Tom made five pitchers of lemonade. Each pitcher had eleven cups of lemonade. How many cups of lemonade did he make in total?**

    A 16   B 50   C 55   D 60

---

3   **Which shape group does not go with the others?**

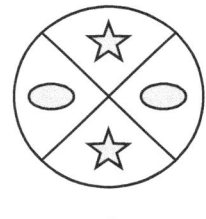    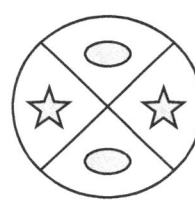

A   B   C   D   E

---

4   **What number should replace the question mark (?) so that all three sets of numbers go together in the same way?**

[2 → 12]   [4 → 24]   [5 → ?]

    A 11   B 1   C 6   D 12   E 30

5   The opposite of typical is _____.

   A confusing   B unusual   C ordinary   D frightening

6   Ana is saving up for a pair of shoes that cost $24. She earns $8 a week by helping her dad with chores. How many weeks will she need to save before she can buy the shoes?

   A 4   B 2   C 3   D 6

7   Which shape group does not go with the others?

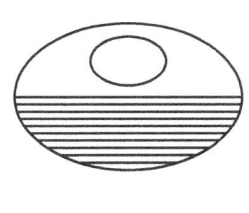   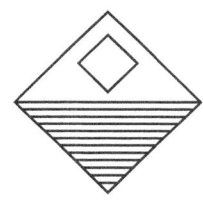   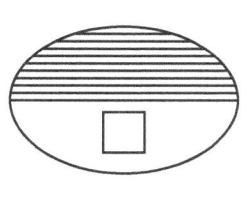      

   A   B   C   D   E

8   What number should replace the question mark (?) so that all three sets of numbers go together in the same way?

   [3, 6, 7]   [4, 8, 9]   [5, 10, ?]

   A 8   B 9   C 12   D 11   E 13

9 The opposite of fragile is _____.

    A delicate   B expensive   C strong   D breakable

---

10 Which choice makes the second set of pictures go together in the same way as the first set?

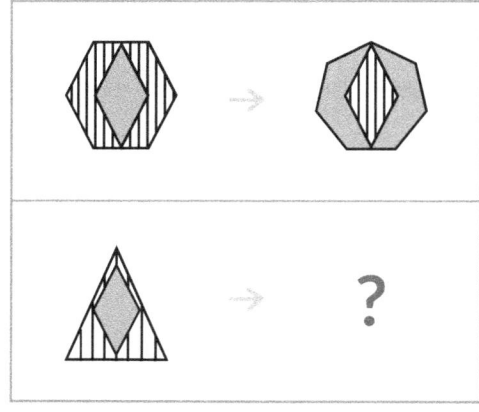

   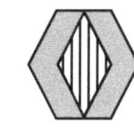      

    A   B   C   D

---

11 What number should replace the question mark (?) so that all three sets of numbers go together in the same way?

[4, 7, 10]   [18, 21, 24]   [10, ?, 16]

    A 13   B 12   C 3   D 11   E 15

---

12 The numbers in the below box go together in a certain way. Which answer choice would replace the question mark?

15	23	31
19	27	35
16	24	?

    A 21   B 28   C 16   D 32

21 The words below need to be arranged to make the best sentence. Which letter would the last word of the sentence begin with? Here are the words:

sunlight   through   filtered   the   leaves   of   tree   a

A T   B S   C A   D F

22 Which answer choice best completes the sentence?

The photographer decided to _____ the settings after she _____ that the images were too dark.

A keep, realized   B adjust, noticed   C ignore, spotted   D write, observed

23 A kitchen must always have _____.

A cabinets   B a freezer   C a sink   D a microwave

24 What number should replace the question mark (?) so that all three sets of numbers go together in the same way?

[43 → 24]   [51 → 32]   [32 → ?]

A 21   B 14   C 12   D 23   E 13

25 The words below need to be arranged to make the best sentence. Which letter would the <u>first</u> word of the sentence begin with? Here are the words:

path   the   twisting   bikers   rode   ten

(A) P   (B) B   (C) T   (D) M

---

26 Which answer choice best completes the sentence?

To _____ a peaceful community, it is _____ to respect others.

(A) keep, realized   (B) notice, nice   (C) ignore, optional   (D) create, necessary

---

27 Maria went to the market. She bought some apples, 15 oranges, and 7 pears. She bought 35 pieces of fruit total. How many apples did she buy?

(A) 13   (B) 20   (C) 35   (D) 14

---

28 A hospital must always have _____.

(A) patients   (B) stairs   (C) doctors   (D) ambulances

---

29 What number comes next in the series?

6   7   9   12   16   21   27   ?

○ 39   ○ 34   ○ 40   ○ 32   ○ 45

30 The words below need to be arranged to make the best sentence. Which letter would the last word of the sentence begin with? Here are the words:

damaged   attempted   bridge   people   cross   a   to   badly

A A   B P   C C   D B

31 Which answer choice best completes the sentence?

Our town has around 5,000 people, but this is only an _____, not an _____ number.

A opinion, identical   B accurate, noticed   C estimate, exact   D addition, abstract

32 Lisa sent out 5 invitations for her sleepover. Her sister invited 3 more friends. If Lisa wants each guest to have 4 slices of pizza, how many slices of pizza will she need?

A 36   B 12   C 32   D 8

33 A bakery must always have _____.

A bread   B an oven   C cakes   D customers

34 What number comes next in the series?

10   11   16   17   22   23   28   ?

30   24   39   33   29

35 Which answer choice makes the second set of words go together in the same way that the first set does?

awful → bad : great → ?

A terrific   B quality   C good   D surprising

36 Which answer choice makes the second set of words go together in the same way that the first set does?

flowers → bouquet : minutes → ?

A clock   B seconds   C watch   D hour

37 Which word does not go with the others?

A potato   B radish   C onion   D carrot   E lettuce

38 Which word does not go with the others?

A triangle   B sphere   C pentagon   D square   E circle

39 The words in the below box go together in a certain way. Which answer choice would replace the question mark?

join	appear	raise
split	disappear	?

A flat   B climb   C increase   D lower

40 Which answer choice makes the second set of words go together in the same way that the first set does?

pretty → beautiful : small → ?

A tiny   B medium   C size   D large

41 Which answer choice makes the second set of words go together in the same way that the first set does?

liquid → solid : bright → ?

A light   B dim   C shine   D laser

42 Which word does not go with the others?

A bay   B stream   C rain   D sea   E pond

43 Which word does not go with the others?

A fairy   B elf   C astronaut   D witch   E wizard

44 The words in the below box go together in a certain way. Which answer choice would replace the question mark?

octagon	elf	ink
oak	each	?

A igloo   B insect   C ice   D inch

45 The words in the below box go together in a certain way. Which answer choice would replace the question mark?

thermometer	ruler	scale
temperature	length	?

Ⓐ time   Ⓑ weight   Ⓒ width   Ⓓ weather

46 Which choice makes the second set of pictures go together in the same way as the first set?

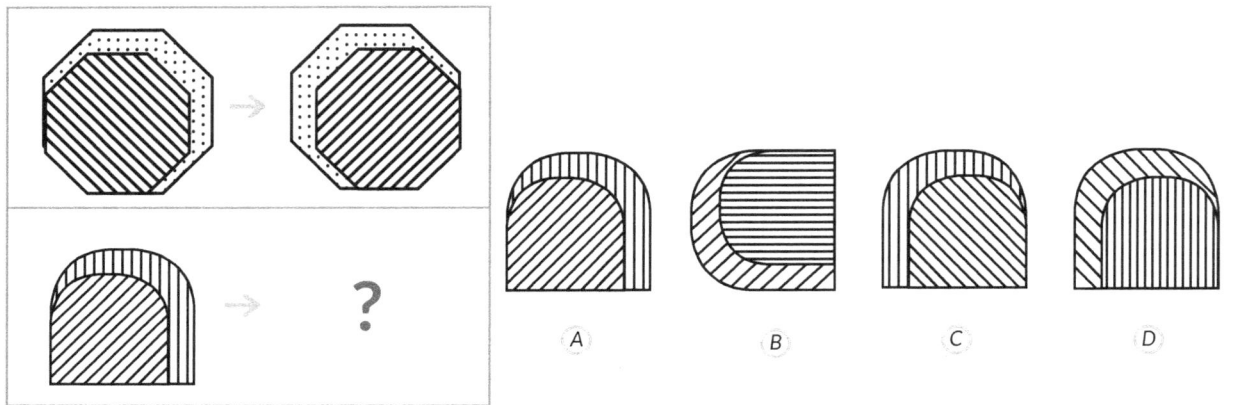

47 Which shape does not go with the others?

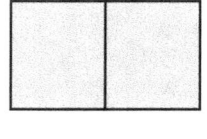   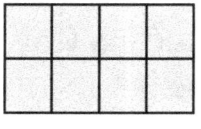   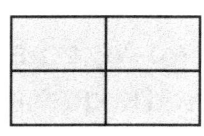   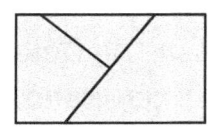   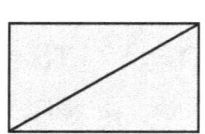

A   B   C   D   E

48 What number comes next in the series?

1 ½   2   2 ½   3   3 ½   4   4 ½   ?

◯ 4 ¾   ◯ 5   ◯ 5 ½   ◯ 6   ◯ 3 ½

49 The words in the below box go together in a certain way. Which answer choice would replace the question mark?

mammal	bird	reptile
monkey	bald eagle	?

A snail   B spider   C beetle   D lizard

50 Which choice makes the second set of pictures go together in the same way as the first set?

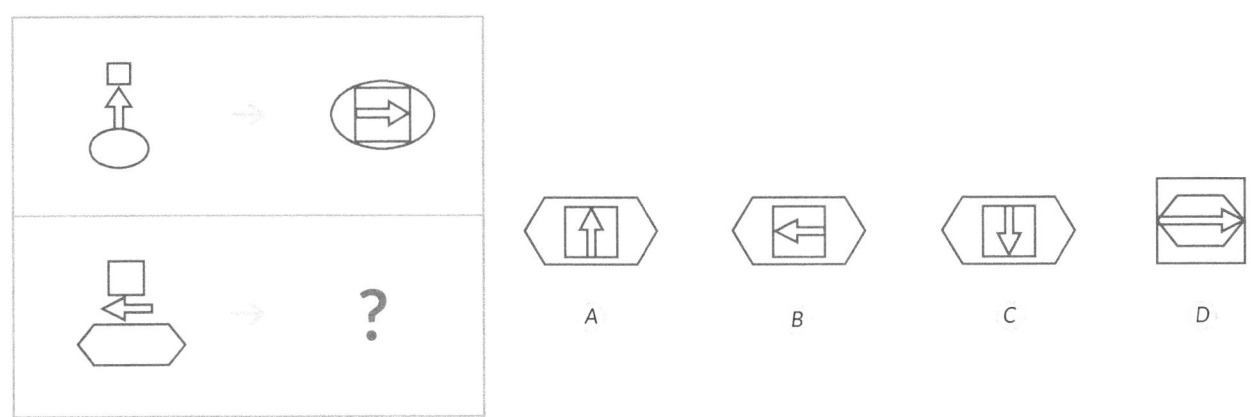

A   B   C   D

51 Which shape does not go with the others?

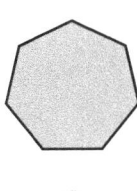

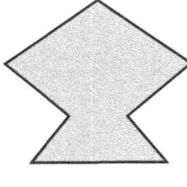

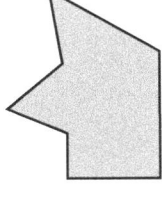

A   B   C   D   E

52 The numbers in the below box go together in a certain way. Which answer choice would replace the question mark?

23	17	11
15	9	3
?	10	4

A 23   B 9   C 7   D 16

53 What comes next in the series?

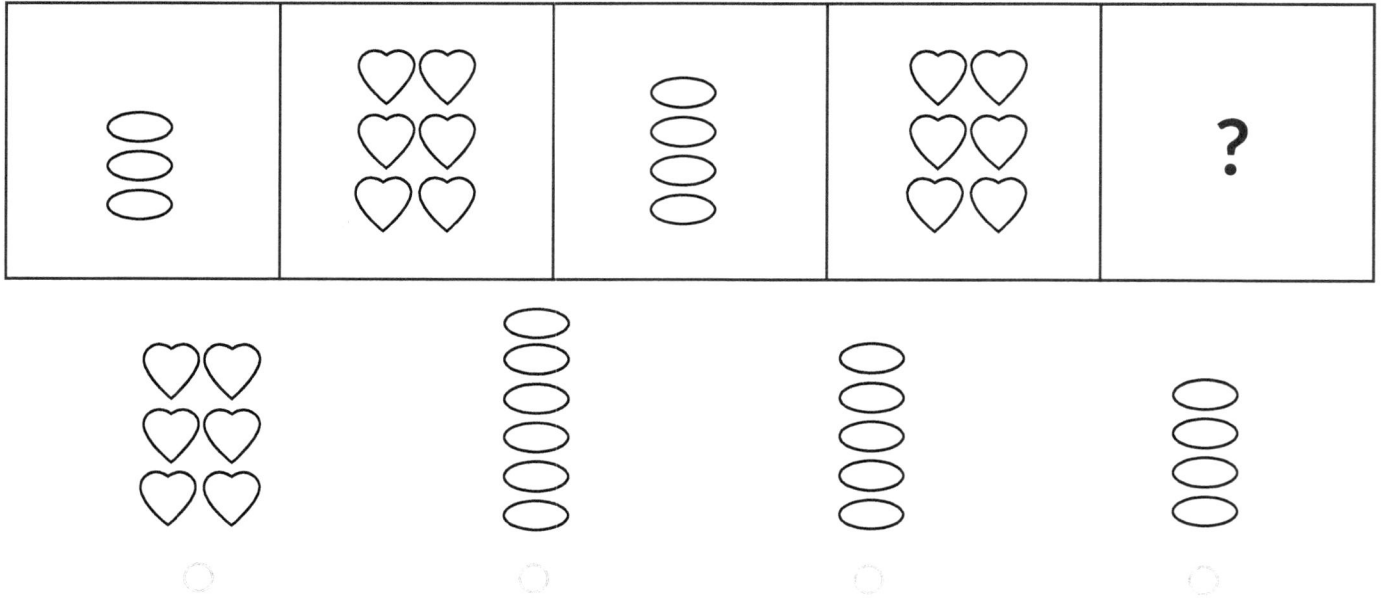

55   Which answer choice would replace the question mark?

29	37	35
?	50	48

A 52   B 42   C 32   D 37

56   The objects in the boxes go together in a certain way.
What goes in the empty box?

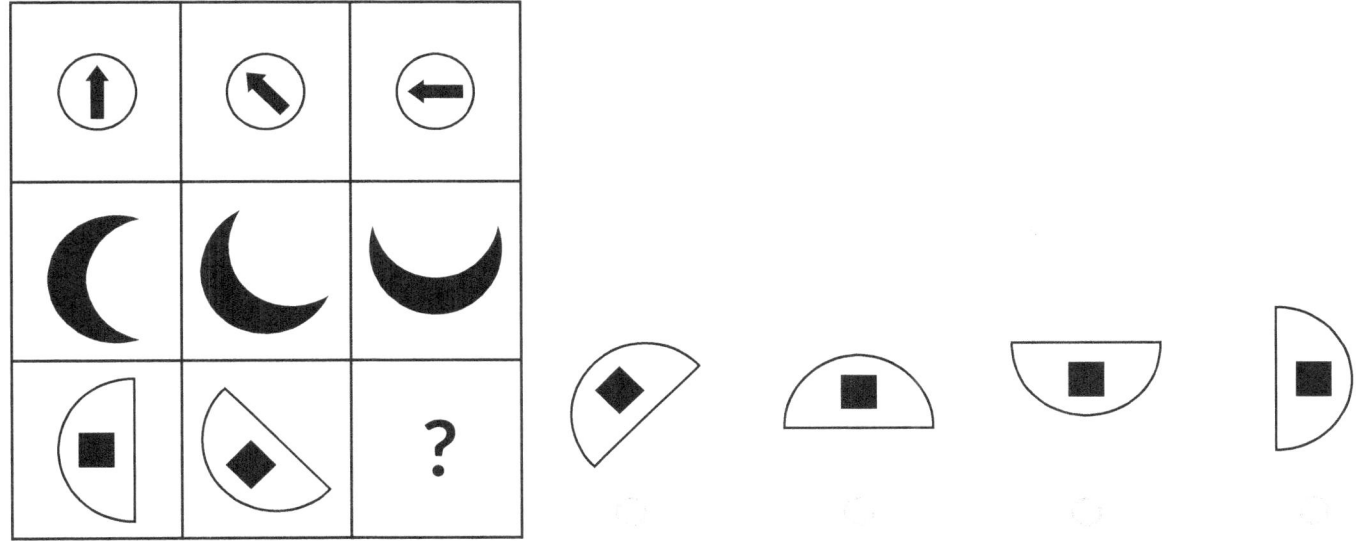

57   What comes next in the series?

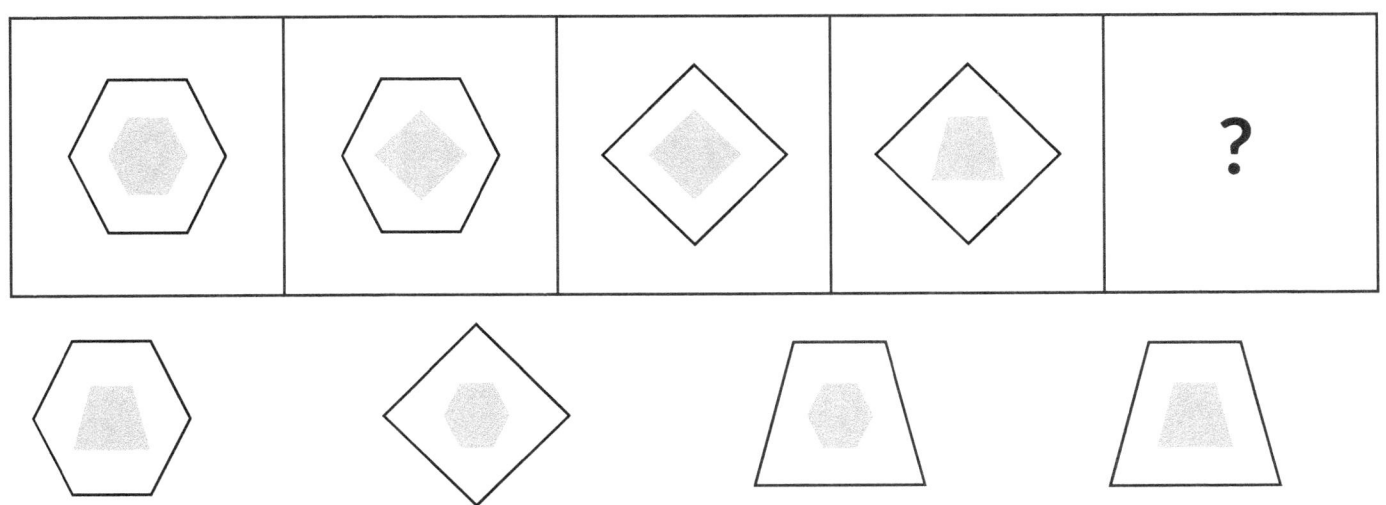

58 The objects in the boxes go together in a certain way.
What goes in the empty box?

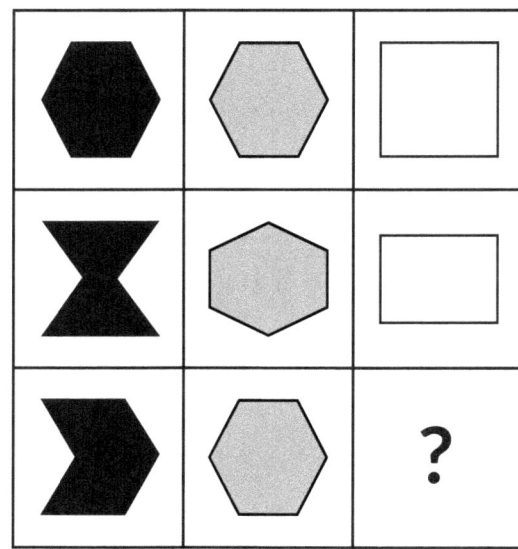

 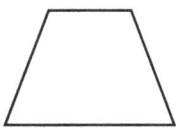 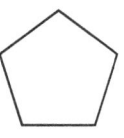 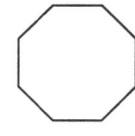

59 The objects in the boxes go together in a certain way.
What goes in the empty box?

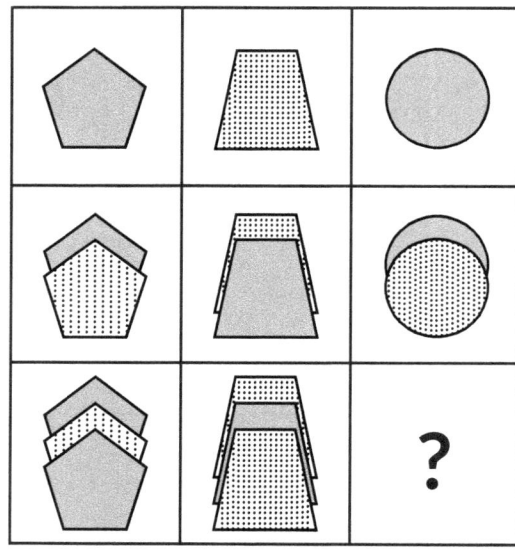

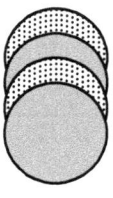   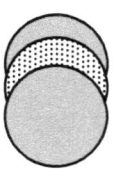

60 What number comes next in the series?

1   3   9   27   ?

○ 54   ○ 30   ○ 81   ○ 61   ○ 3

61 The objects in the boxes go together in a certain way.
What goes in the empty box?

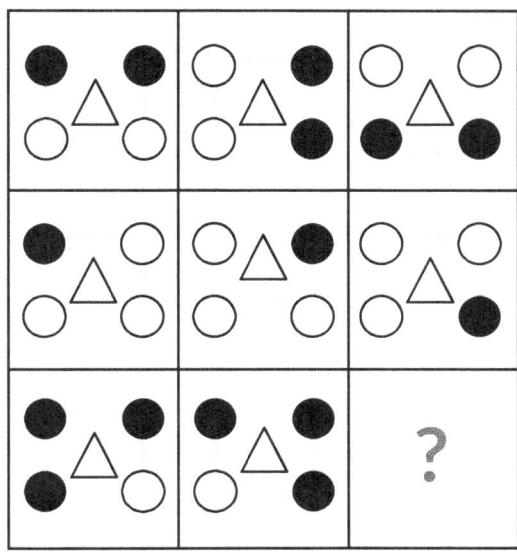

      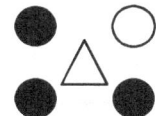   

62 What comes next in the series?

63 What number comes next in the series?

2   21   40   59   78   ?

80   107   19   87   97

ANSWER KEY FOR PRACTICE TEST 1 (WORKBOOK FORMAT)

Antonyms

-1. C: To gather means to bring things or people together. To scatter means to spread things apart or in different directions.
-2. B: To expand means to make something larger or grow in size. To shrink means to make something smaller.
-3. A: Victory means to win a fight or a competition. Defeat means to lose a fight or a competition.
-4. D: Temporary means lasting for only a limited period of time. Permanent means lasting forever.

Sentence Completion

-5. B: powerful = strong, full of power
-6. B: demanding = needing a lot of effort, energy, and time
-7. D: immense = very large
-8. B: patience = waiting calmly without getting upset; habitat = natural home or environment where an animal or plant lives

Sentence Arrangement

-9. C. Sentence: I was running late for the bus.
-10. A. Sentence: The rain fell outside his window.
-11. D. Sentence: The crowd waited patiently for the train.
-12. A. Sentence: Wind carried fallen leaves across a field.

Arithmetic Reasoning

-13. D: 14 + 28 = 42 (Note that the question asked only about Maria's team. Only Maria and Jason are on Maria's team.)
-14. C: 3 + 1 + 2 = 6 (Note that the question asked only about pies.)
-15. B: 5 + 2 = 7 (Note that the question has info we don't need - how many balloons Jamie got.)
-16. A: 8 x 4 = 32 (8 pencils multiplied by 4 boxes = 32)

Logical Selection

-17. B: Every car must have a steering wheel to be driven. A car may have a radio, heat, or A/C, but these are not 100% necessary.
-18. D: Every chair must have legs to stand on. A chair may have arms, cushions, or a backrest, but are not 100% necessary.
-19. A: Every mountain must have a peak to be classified as a mountain. It may have snow, trees, or rocks, but the peak is necessary.
-20. A: Every road must have an end. A road may have signs, lanes, or pavement, but it must eventually have an end.

Verbal Analogies

-21. B: Opposites
-22. D: People have hair, which on animals (like dogs and cats), compares to fur. People have feet, which on animals (like dogs and cats), compares to paws.
-23. C: A house's top part is the attic. A mountain's top part is the peak.
-24. B: A unit of measurement for weight is a pound. A unit of measurement for temperature is a degree.

Verbal Classification

-25. B: types of colors ("color" is not correct, because the word must be a <u>type</u> of color)
-26. E: emotions you feel when you are happy (a smile is an action, not an emotion)
-27. D: things that come in pairs (also, you can eat fruit; the others cannot be eaten)
-28. A: things used to keep track of time

Verbal Matrix

-29. C: first letter stays at the beginning of the word (d on top & l on bottom), second letter is doubles (e on top, o on bottom), the third letter is removed (d on top, l on bottom), the last letter stays at the end of the word (r on top, k on bottom)
-30. D: final word is a combo of the letter groups, with the second letter group ahead of the first
-31. A. down the columns (starting with "between," "cold," etc.), the words are in alphabetical order
-32. B: down the columns, the top word & bottom word are opposites

Figure Classification

-33. A: wavy lines inside shape   -34. D: diagonal line goes from upper left to lower right
-35. C: shape group is a large outer shape with an inner shape (that is the same shape)
-36. C: 1/4 of shape is filled with lines (not dots)

Figure Analogies

-37. A: designs/colors of small & large shapes switch
-38. C: bottom shape moves to top & the other 2 move down -or- dotted section changes to gray; black section changes to dotted; gray section changes to black
-39. D: arrow group rotates 90° clockwise and 1 arrow is added.
-40. D: top left & bottom right switch

Figure Series

-41. B: 2 black parallelograms rotate clockwise around the shape group
-42. D: the first shape in the group moves to the end

Pattern Matrix

-43. B: down columns/across rows is one of each: star, square, up arrow
-44. A: down columns/across rows is one less circle
-45. C: down columns/across rows figure rotates 90 degrees clockwise

Numeric Matrix

-46. D: across the rows: +18; down the columns: -12
-47. A: across rows: 2 different operations, -9, then +3; down columns: +10
-48. B: across rows: 2 different operations, +9, then +3; down columns: +12
-49. D: across rows: -8, then +15; down columns: -11

Numeric Inferences

-50. E: divide by 2   -51. D: subtract 8
-52. C: in each group, the second number is the number in the hundreds place of the first number
-53. C: in each group of 3 numbers, the first number is multiplied by 2, then this answer is added to 2; 3 x 2 = 6, 6 + 2 = 8; 5 x 2 = 10, 10 + 2 = 12; 6 x 2 = 12, 12 + 2 = 14

Numeric Series

-54. D: +1, +2, +1. +2, etc.   -55. D: +2, +3, +2, +3, etc.
-56. C: in places 1,3,5 there's a "0"; in places 2,4,6 add +1   -57. A: -2, +1, -2, +1, etc.

ANSWER KEY FOR PRACTICE TEST 2

- Note: At the end of each explanation is the OLSAT® question type in gray font (Antonyms,

  Sentence Arrangement, Arithmetic Reasoning, Figure Analogies, etc.).

-1. D. Decrease means to make something smaller in size or amount. Increase means to make something larger. Antonyms
-2. A. Correct sentence: The exhausted runners finished a marathon. Sentence Arrangement
-3. C. If Ben gives away all of the marbles except 8 marbles, that means Ben has 8 marbles left. Arithmetic Reasoning
-4. B. One arrow point is removed. Figure Analogies
-5. A. Frequent means happening often. Rare means happening infrequently (the opposite of frequently). Antonyms
-6. D. Every plane must have wings to fly. The other things are not needed to fly. Logical Selection
-7. E. things used for cutting Verbal Classification
-8. B. adjectives used to describe being tired/sleepy Verbal Classification
-9. E. bottom shape has rotated 90 degrees counterclockwise (to the left) Figure Classification
-10. B. Correct sentence: Students neatly organized papers on a table. Sentence Arrangement
-11. B. If Mr. Lee baked 7 fewer cakes than Mrs. Smith, and Mrs. Smith baked 12 cakes, then Mr. Lee baked 5 cakes. 12 - 7 = 5. Arithmetic Reasoning
-12. D. From left to right, larger shape has 1 more side, smaller shape has 1 more side; colors of large & small shape reverse white/gray Figure Analogies
-13. C. across rows: -5, -5; down columns: +5 Numeric Matrix
-14. B. curious = eager to learn or explore new things (the other choices, "silent" and "calm" would not describe a puppy who's barking) Sentence Completion
-15. A. first letter stays at the beginning of the word ("m" on top & "f" on bottom), second letter is doubled ("e" on top, "o" on bottom), the third letter is removed ("m" on top, "f" on bottom), the last letter stays at the end ("t" on top, "d" on bottom) Verbal Matrix
-16. D. diagonal lines going from lower left corner to upper right corner Figure Classification
-17. C. ancient = from the very distant past Sentence Completion
-18. C. subtract 7 Numeric Inferences
-19. C. Correct sentence: Five hikers climbed up the steep mountain peak. Sentence Arrangement
-20. D. If Carlos prepared 4 trays, and each tray had 9 brownies, he prepared a total of: 4 × 9 = 36 brownies. Arithmetic Reasoning
-21. D. Every desert must have dryness. The definition of a desert is an area that receives very little rainfall, making it dry. Logical Selection
-22. B. A ruler is used to measure length. A compass is used to measure direction (by showing which way is north, etc.). Verbal Analogies
-23. C. A carriage provides a slower form of transport than a car. A car has a motor. Both usually have 4 wheels. A bicycle provides a slower form of transport than a motorcycle. A motorcycle has a motor. Both usually have 2 wheels. Verbal Analogies
-24. A. Correct sentence: A student finished his reports and submitted them. Sentence Arrangement
-25. C. The definition of a forest is a large area covered primarily with trees. Logical Selection
-26. B. A mechanic would fix an engine. A plumber would fix a drain. Verbal Analogies
-27. A. Bread is made from grain. Paper is made from a tree. Verbal Analogies

-28. D. down the columns, the words are in alphabetical order Verbal Matrix
-29. C. maximum = the most possible; minimum = the least possible Antonyms
-30. D. rival = competitor Sentence Completion
-31. C. If Ben earns $9 a week, and the book costs $18, figure out how many weeks he needs to save by dividing the total cost of the book by how much he earns per week. $18 ÷ $9 = 2 weeks. Arithmetic Reasoning
-32. B. Every volcano must have magma beneath the surface. Magma is the molten rock that can erupt from the volcano. Logical Selection
-33. A. +8 Numeric Series
-34. A. Rarely means something happens infrequently. Often means something happens frequently, which is the opposite of rarely. Antonyms
-35. D. landscape = the land/scenery of a particular area Sentence Completion
-36. D. mammals Verbal Classification
-37. B. liquids Verbal Classification
-38. E. 3 down arrows & 1 up arrow Figure Classification
-39. C. multiply by 2 Numeric Series
-40. A. down the columns, the first top & bottom words are opposites Verbal Matrix
-41. C. small white shape turns dark & rotates 90° Figure Analogies
-42. B. 1 of 3 shapes must have: black, dotted lines, or solid horizontal lines Figure Classification
-43. D. +1, +2, +1, +2, etc. Numeric Series
-44. B. down the columns, the words begin with the same letter Verbal Matrix
-45. D. larger shape the color of smaller shape Figure Analogies
-46. E. the second number is the number in the tens place of the first number Numeric Inferences
-47. D. -1, -2, -3, -4, -5, -6, -7, -8 Numeric Series
-48. A. across rows: -4; down columns: +7 Numeric Matrix
-49. D. shape group rotates 90 degrees clockwise Figure Series
-50. B. across rows: +11, then +4; down columns: +14 Numeric Matrix
-51. C. top shape moves to the bottom Figure Series
-52. D. across rows: +9; down columns: +10 Numeric Matrix
-53. A. in each box, another diagonal of circles gets filled in Figure Series
-54. B. each row/column must have a box with 1 of each: 1, 2, 3 circles; the boxes with 1 & 2 circles must have the circles on the left Pattern Matrix
-55. C. each time number of stars decreases by 1 / number of hearts increases by 1 Figure Series
-56. A. across rows, shape rotates like this - box 2: 180°, box 3: 90° clockwise Pattern Matrix
-57. B. across the rows, the last box has an outer diamond with dotted lines & each row/column must have a circle, triangle, and star as an inner shape Pattern Matrix
-58. A. 2 sections with dotted lines move counterclockwise around circle Figure Series
-59. E. divide by 3 Numeric Inferences
-60. D. each row/column must have a group of 1 circle, 2 circles, 3 circles -and- circle(s) with gray, stripes, dots Pattern Matrix
-61. C. in each row, there is a pentagon + star together; the pentagon & star separated are opposite colors from the pentagon + star together Pattern Matrix
-62. A. half Numeric Inferences

ANSWER KEY FOR PRACTICE TEST 3

-1. B. Scarce means in short supply. Abundant means plenty or more than enough. Antonyms
-2. C. If Tom made 5 pitchers, and each pitcher had 11 cups of lemonade, he made a total of 5 × 11 = 55 cups of lemonade. Arithmetic Reasoning
-3. D. inside circle are 2 pairs of the same shape that are across from each other Figure Classification
-4. E. multiply by 6 Numeric Inferences
-5. B. Typical means usual or expected. Unusual means out of the ordinary. Antonyms
-6. C. If Ana earns $8 a week and the shoes cost $24, we can find how many weeks she needs to save by dividing the total cost of the shoes by how much she earns per week. $24 ÷ $8 = 3 weeks Arithmetic Reasoning
-7. C. the white shape is a smaller version of the large shape that's divided; the large shape has a white section & a section with horizontal lines Figure Classification
-8. D. in each group of 3 numbers, the first number is multiplied by 2, then this answer is added to 1; 3 x 2 = 6, 6 + 1 = 7; 4 x 2 = 8, 8 + 1 = 9; 5 x 2 = 10, 10 + 1 = 11 Numeric Inferences
-9. C. Fragile means easily broken or delicate. Strong means tough or not easily damaged. Antonyms
-10. D. larger shape gains 1 side & design of larger/smaller shape switch Figure Analogies
-11. A. in each group of 3 numbers, 3 is added to the first number, then 3 is added to the middle number Numeric Inferences
-12. D. across rows, add 8; down columns, add 4, then subtract 3 Numeric Matrix
-13. D. Proceed means to continue or move forward. The opposite is "stop." Antonyms
-14. B. White shape increases & light gray shape decreases with smaller version on top of larger version Figure Analogies
-15. B. divide by 6 Numeric Inferences
-16. C. begins w/1, every other number is 1; then, starting with 10, every other number is +5 Numeric Series
-17. A. She continues with her science project. Sentence Arrangement
-18. B. Every table must have legs to stand. Logical Selection
-19. A. down the columns, the top & bottom words are opposites Verbal Matrix
-20. C: add 9 Numeric Inferences
-21. A. Correct sentence: Sunlight filtered through the leaves of a tree. -or- The sunlight filtered through leaves of a tree. (With either sentence the last word is the same.) Sentence Arrangement
-22. B. adjust = change; notice = to see something & be aware of it Sentence Completion
-23. C. Every kitchen must have a sink for cleaning. Logical Selection
-24. E. -19 Numeric Inferences
-25. C. Correct sentence: Ten bikers rode the twisting path. Sentence Arrangement
-26. D. create = to make something happen or exist; necessary = something that's needed for a purpose or a reason Sentence Completion
-27. A. First, figure out how many oranges (15) and pears (7) Mrs. Green bought. 15 + 7 = 22. Next, subtract the total of oranges and pears (22) from the total number of fruits (35) she bought. 35 - 22 = 13 Arithmetic Reasoning
-28. C. Every hospital must have doctors. Hospitals may not always have ambulances, patients, or beds, but doctors are necessary for medical care. Logical Selection
-29. B. +1, +2, +3, +4, +5, +6, etc. Numeric Series
-30. D. People attempted to cross a badly damaged bridge. Sentence Arrangement
-31. C. estimate = a guess/idea, not exact; exact = completely correct Sentence Completion
-32. C. First, figure out how many people were invited altogether: add number of people Lisa invited (5) to number of people her sister invited (3). 5 + 3 = 8. Next, multiply 8 by 4 (each guest will have 4 slices of pizza). 8 × 4 = 32 Arithmetic Reasoning

-33. B. Every bakery must have ovens. A bakery may not always have cakes, bread, or customers, but ovens are essential for baking. Logical Selection
-34. E. +1, +5, +1, +5, etc. Numeric Series
-35. C. Awful describes something very bad. Great describes something very good. Verbal Analogies
-36. D. Flowers are what make up a bouquet. Minutes are what make up hours. Verbal Analogies
-37. E. root vegetables Verbal Classification
-38. B. 2-D shapes (a sphere is a 3-D shape) Verbal Classification
-39. D. down the columns, the top & bottom words are opposites Verbal Matrix
-40. A. The second word, beautiful, means very pretty. Tiny (the correct answer) means very small. Verbal Analogies
-41. B. Liquid is the opposite of solid. Bright is the opposite of dim. Verbal Analogies
-42. C. bodies of water Verbal Classification
-43. C. make-believe/fantasy characters Verbal Classification
-44. C. down the columns, the top word has a short vowel of the word's first letter & the bottom word has a long vowel of the word's first letter Verbal Matrix
-45. B. down the columns, the top word is used to measure the bottom word Verbal Matrix
-46. C. inside smaller shape moves from left to right & direction of lines switch Figure Analogies
-47. D. shape parts are divided equally -or- are symmetrical Figure Classification
-48. B. add 1/2 Numeric Series
-49. D. down columns, top is the animal class & bottom is an animal in that class Verbal Matrix
-50. A. Top shape goes inside bottom shape & gets bigger. Middle shape goes inside & rotates 90° clockwise. Figure Analogies
-51. C. 7-sided shapes Figure Classification
-52. D. across rows: -6, then -6; down columns: -8, then +1 Numeric Matrix
-53. C. in every other shape group (groups 1-3-5), amount of ovals increases by 1 Figure Series
-54. A. across rows: +5, then +3; down columns: +9 Numeric Matrix
-55. B. across rows: +8, then -2; down columns: +13 Numeric Matrix
-56. C. across rows: shape group rotates 45 degrees counterclockwise Pattern Matrix
-57. D. every other shape group (groups 1-3-5) has a same smaller & larger shape Figure Series
-58. B. across rows & down columns, shapes have 6 sides, 6 sides, 4 sides Pattern Matrix
-59. D. across the rows, the number of shapes is the same, but the design of the shapes alternates gray-dots-gray; down the columns, 1 more of the same shape is added & the design alternates gray-dots-gray (column 1&3) and dots-gray-dots (column 2) Pattern Matrix
-60. C. multiply by 3
-61. A. the black dots go around the triangle clockwise, moving 1 circle each time & the horizontal gray line switches from top to bottom Pattern Matrix
-62. C. the "pac-man" shape at beginning moves to end & dotted line switches from bottom/top Figure Series
-63. E. add 19 Number Series

Ready for test day?

Check out more OLSAT® books at

www.GatewayGifted.com

Grade 2

Grade 1